THE
100 GREATEST
STOCK MARKET WINNERS
OF THE
PAST 15 YEARS

DAILY GRAPHS

A DIVISION OF WILLIAM O'NEIL & CO.

© Copyright 1977 William O'Neil & Co., Inc.

All Rights Reserved

P.O. Box 24933, Los Angeles, Ca. 90024 (213) 820-2583

CONTENTS

	PAGE
FOREWARD	3
HOW TO READ	4
ASA LTD.	5
ADAMS – MILLIS	6
AMERICAN RESEARCH & DEVELOPMENT	7
AMREP	8
ATLANTIC RICHFIELD CO.	9
ATLAS CONS MINING & DEVELOPMENT	10
BAUSCH & LOMB	11
BEST PRODUCTS INC.	12
BRANIFF	13
BURROUGHS	14
CALIFORNIA COMPUTER	15
CARBON INDUSTRIES INC.	16
CHAMPION HOME BUILDERS	17
CHRYSLER	18
CONDEC CORP.	19
CRANE CO.	20
DAYTON HUDSON CORP.	21
DELTA AIRLINES	22
DELTONA	23
DIAMOND SHAMROCK CORP.	24
DIGITAL EQUIPMENT	25
DUPLAN	26
E.SYSTEMS INC.	27
EG & G INCORPORATED	28
ECHLIN MANUFACTURING	29
ECKERD JACK CORP.	30
EDISON BROTHERS STORES	31
ENGELHARD MINING & CHEMICAL	32
FAIRCHILD CAMERA & INSTRUMENT	33
FALCON SEABOARD	34
FEDDERS	35
FOREST CITY ENTERPRISES	36
GENERAL CINEMA CORP.	37
HANDLEMAN	38
HILTON HOTELS	39
HOUSE OF FABRICS	40
HOUSTON OIL & MINERALS	41
HYGRADE FOOD PRODUCTS	42
I-T-E IMPERIAL CORP.	43
JAPAN FUND	44
JEANETTE	45
JIM WALTER	46
KATZ DRUG	47
KAUFMAN & BROAD	48
KNICKERBOCKER TOY CO.	49
KRESGE SS CO.	50
LING-TEMCO-VOUGHT	51
LOEWS	52

	PAGE
MGIC	53
MATTEL	54
MAUL BROTHERS	55
MCDONALDS	56
MELVILLE SHOE CORP.	57
MILTON BRADLEY CO.	58
MONOGRAM	59
MOORE MCCORMACK RES INC.	60
MOTOROLA INC.	61
NATIONAL AIRLINES	62
NATIONAL CHEMSEARCH	63
NATIONAL SEMICONDUCTOR	64
NATOMAS	65
NEW PROCESS	66
OCCIDENTAL PETROLEUM	67
OVERNITE TRANSPORTATION	68
PARVIN DOHRMANN	69
PHILIPS INDUSTRIES	70
PITTSTON CO.	71
PLANT INDUSTRIES	72
POLAROID	73
PRODUCTS RESEARCH & CHEMICAL	74
REDMAN INDUSTRIES	75
ROLLINS	76
RYDER SYSTEM INC.	77
SEA CONTAINERS INC.	78
SIMPLICITY PATTERNS	79
SKYLINE	80
SOLITRON DEVICES	81
SANDSTRAND CORP.	82
SYNTEX	83
TANDY CORPORATION	84
TECHNICARE CORP.	85
TELEX CORP	86
TEXAS OIL & GAS CORP.	87
WHITE CONSOLIDATED INDUSTRIES	88
XEROX	89
ZAPATA NORESS	90
DIGITAL EQUIPMENT	91
MCA	91
MITCHELL ENERGY	91
NATIONAL PRESTO	91
NORTHROP	92
PALL	92
RESORTS INTL. CL. A	92
U.S. SHOE	92
A.E. STALEY	93
TANDY	93
TELEDYNE	93
WOODS PETROLEUM	93

FOREWORD

The stock market is a realistic place where success does not occur by accident. There is always a cause behind every important movement (even though the true causes are not usually understood). We believe observations and study of the objects themselves, i.e., the stocks that actually succeeded best and their characteristics at the time, should enable most of us to make many fundamental discoveries (or at least rearrange some of our preconceived opinions and long held beliefs).

This is not necessarily a collection of the best companies, or of only quality blue chips or growth stocks, but a collection of the stocks that produced the best results in the marketplace during various time periods over the last fifteen years. A stock may have produced outstanding results for one year, five years, or only six months. History does repeat itself at many times and under many different circumstances. The farther back one can see and understand, the more clearly should one be able to see ahead.

The 100 stocks we have selected are presented in two charting formats. Stocks that showed a major move lasting more than one year are displayed on a DATAGRAPHS. These show the weekly price history of a stock plotted on a logarithmic scale and cover a five year period. Stocks showing a "winning move" of twelve months or less are displayed on a DAILY GRAPHS, showing the daily price activity for twelve months on an arithmetic scale.

These 100 stocks possessed many common characteristics. DAILY GRAPHS was subsequently designed to help the user identify these commonalities in his stock analysis. Following are a few of the observations we have noted. We hope you find this collection useful in your day to day dealings in the stock market and wish you success for the future.

1. Major increases and acceleration in quarterly earnings per share were the dominant reason behind the success of almost all of the greatest winners.

2. Seventy percent of the examples had already reported increases of 20% or more in earnings for the quarter prior to their large price increase.

3. The average percent increase in quarterly earnings reported and showing before the move, exceeded 70%.

4. The minority that did not show a major earnings increase prior to their big move usually did so in the following quarter.

5. The average earnings increase shown in the following quarter exceeded 90%.

6. The percent increase in earnings was 2 to 3 times more important than the price earnings ratio as a cause of price increases.

7. Many stocks were selling at low P.E.'s and many were selling at high P.E.'s. The average P.E. was approximately 23 at the stock's early emerging stage and most continued on to expand their P.E.'s to higher levels. The average P.E. for the Dow Jones at the same point was 16. With the exception of cyclical stocks, it appeared that low P.E.'s were due to bear markets and high P.E.'s were due to bull markets and that P.E.'s were more of an effect or result than a basic cause of moves.

8. More than half of the examples were a result of group or industry moves that occurred due to changes within an industry.

9. Only 3% of the companies that produced real results had over 20 million shares outstanding during the period of their success.

10. The outstanding leaders throughout one complete bull market were not usually the leaders in the next bull market unless they began late in the past cycle. Many new names led the way in each new cycle.

11. Many stocks were not necessarily labeled "growth stocks" (at least in the prior five years). Many could be classified as former mediocre performers where an important change had occurred, i.e., new products or new management.

12. Most of the outstanding successes showed a period of greater relative strength than the general market before their major move occurred.

13. Important volume indications at a few key points occurred prior to the movement of many of the examples.

14. Most of the major moves were preceded by correction and consolidation areas as well as general market corrections in many cases.

15. The average time period movements lasted from their emerging stage till the peak was 17 months.

HOW TO READ HISTORICAL MODELS

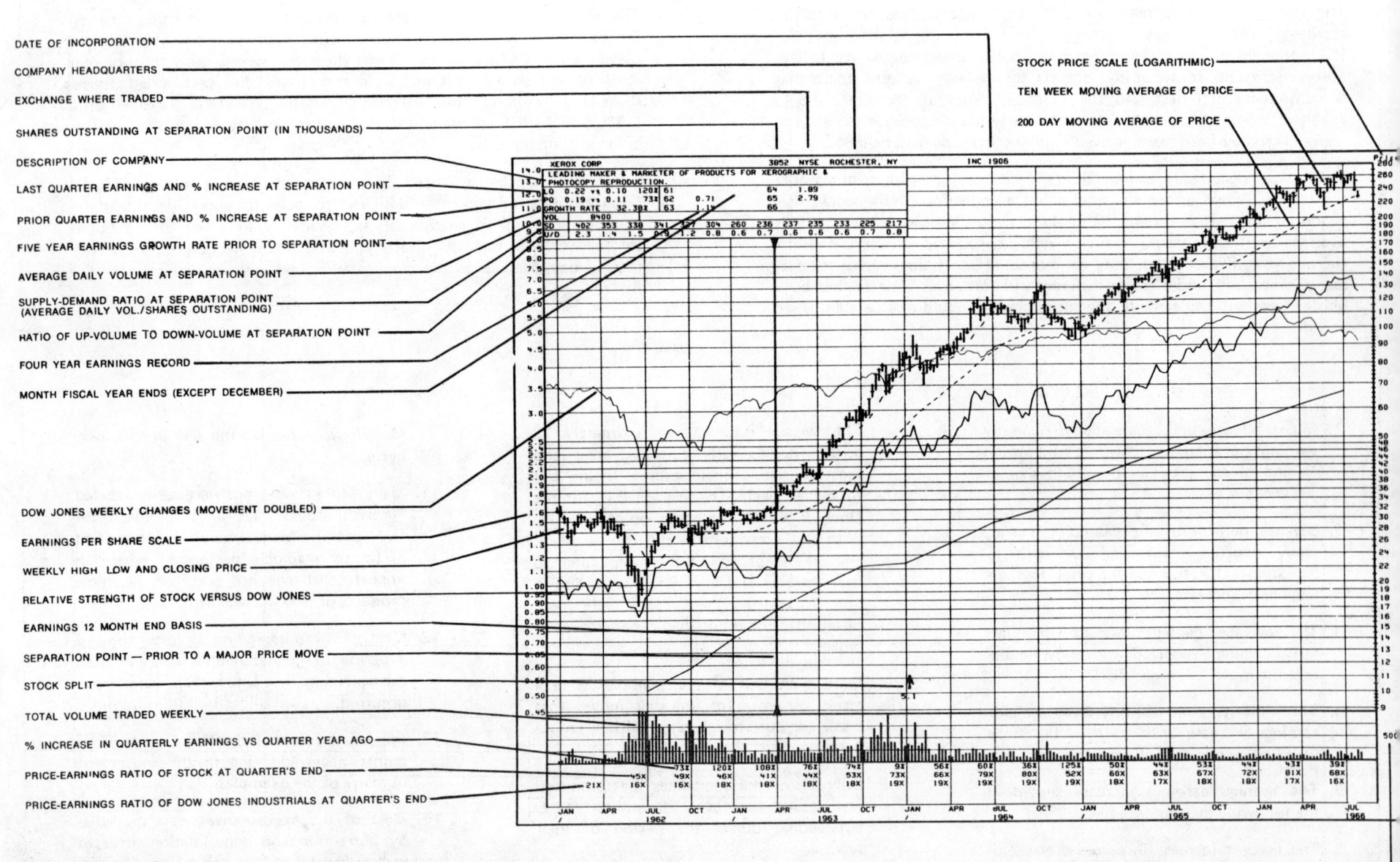

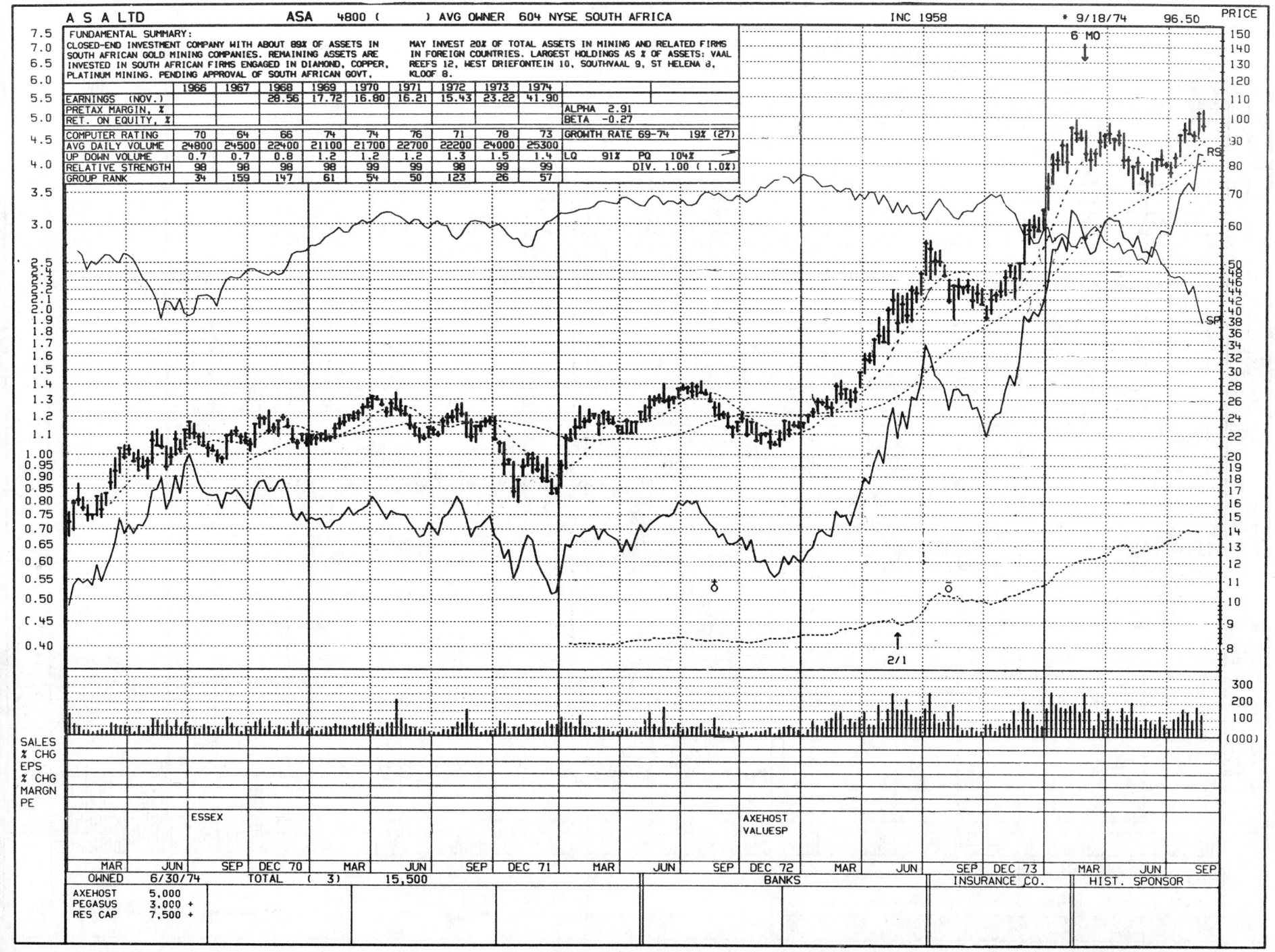

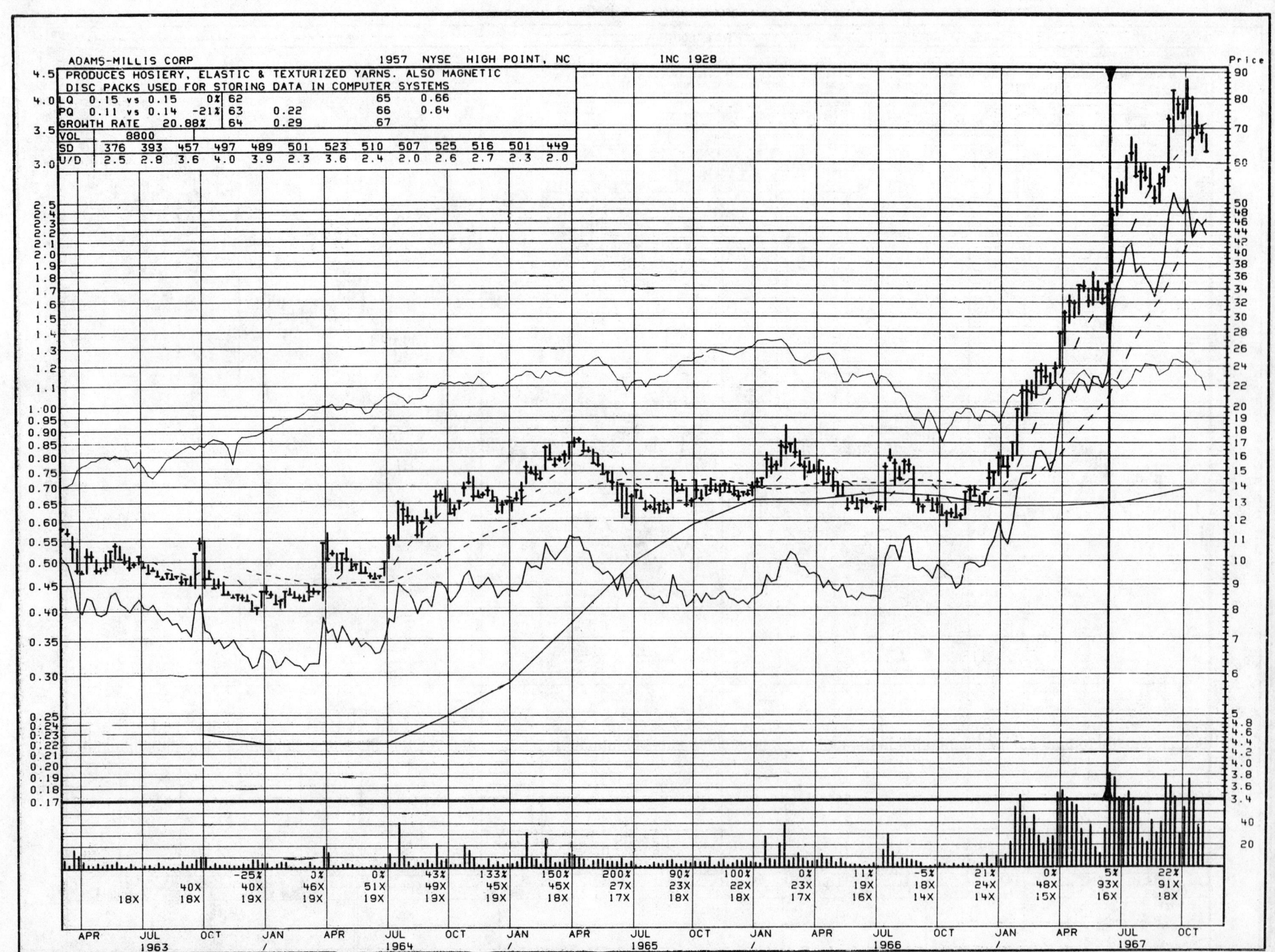

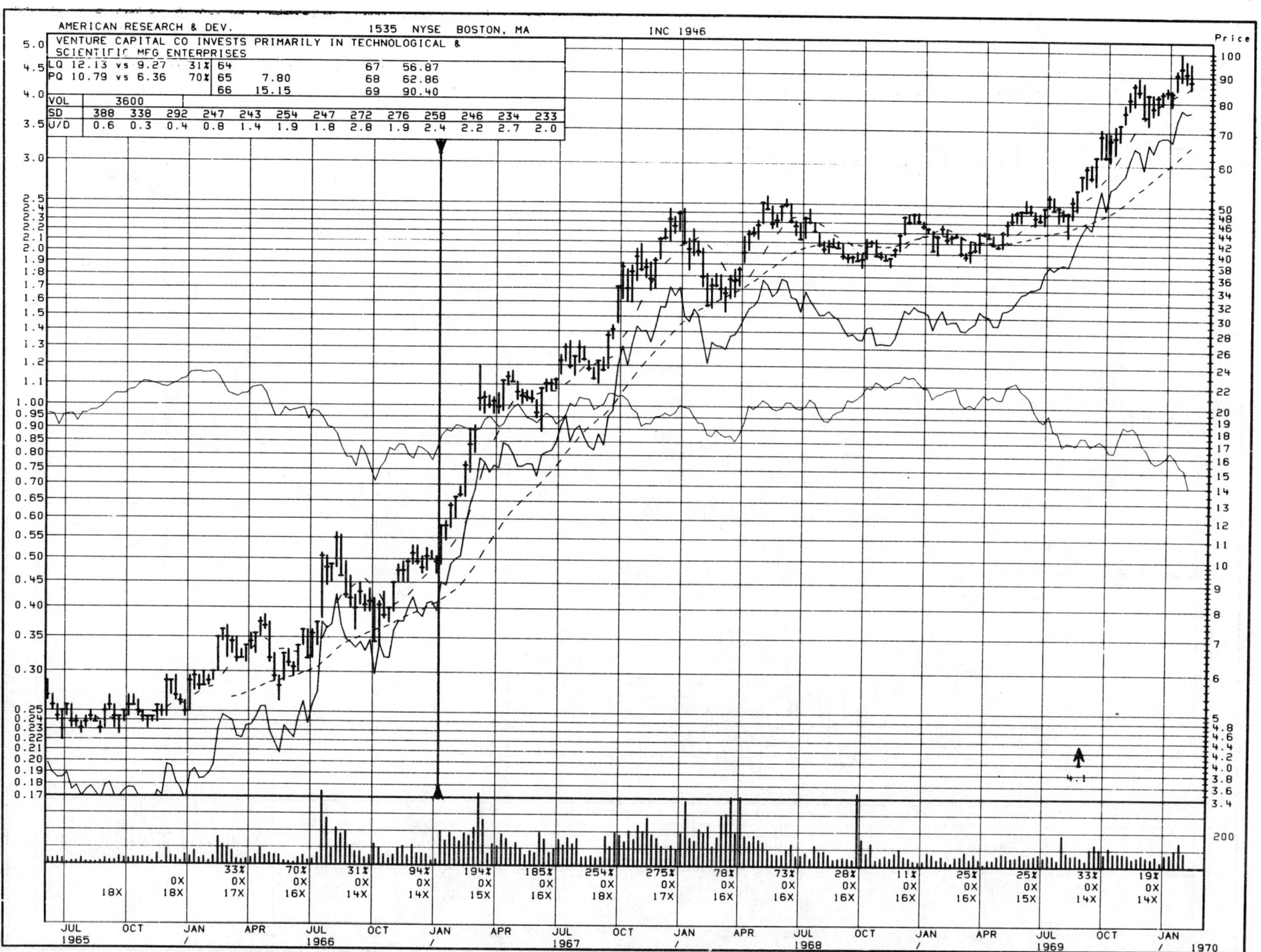

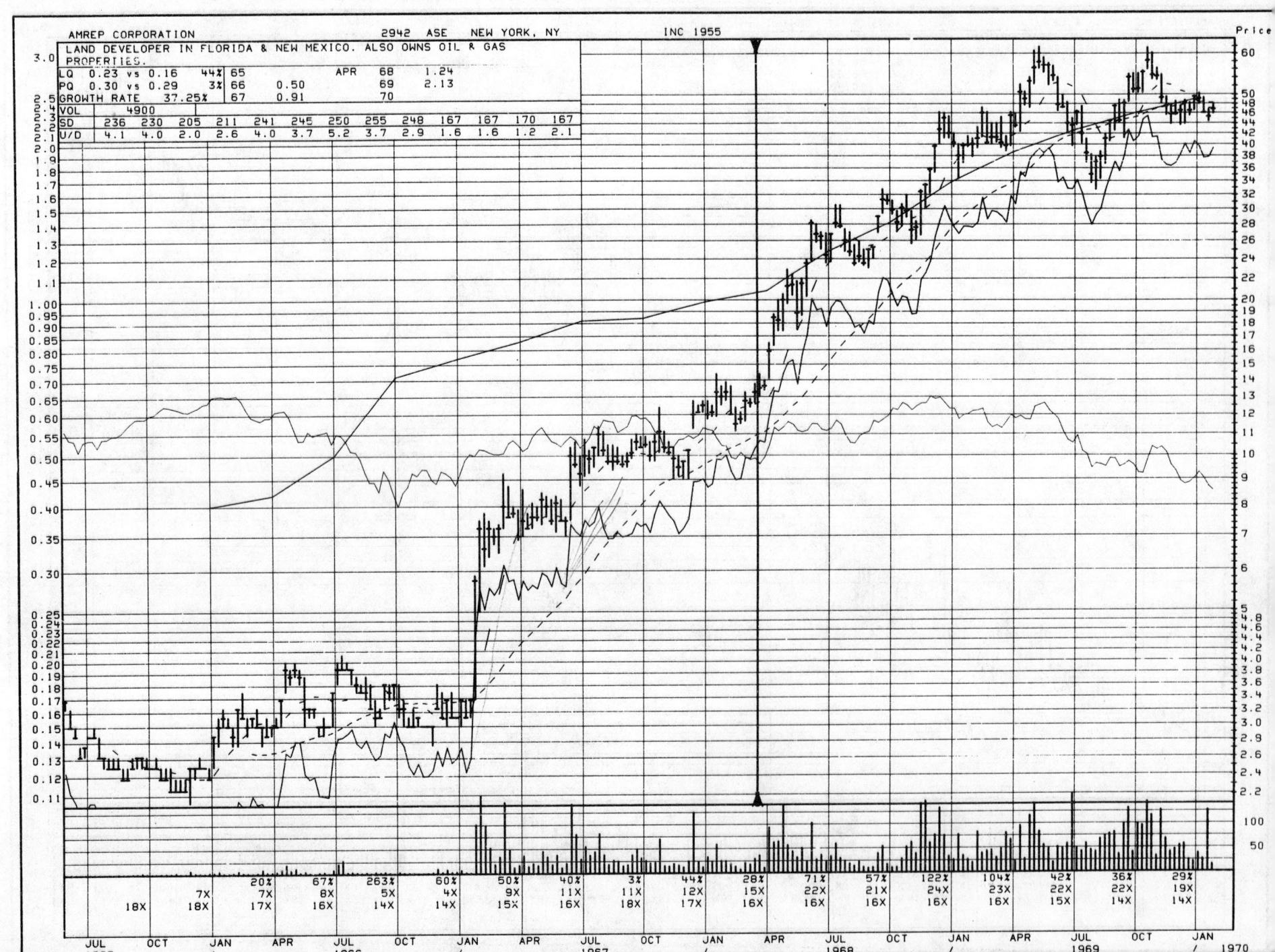

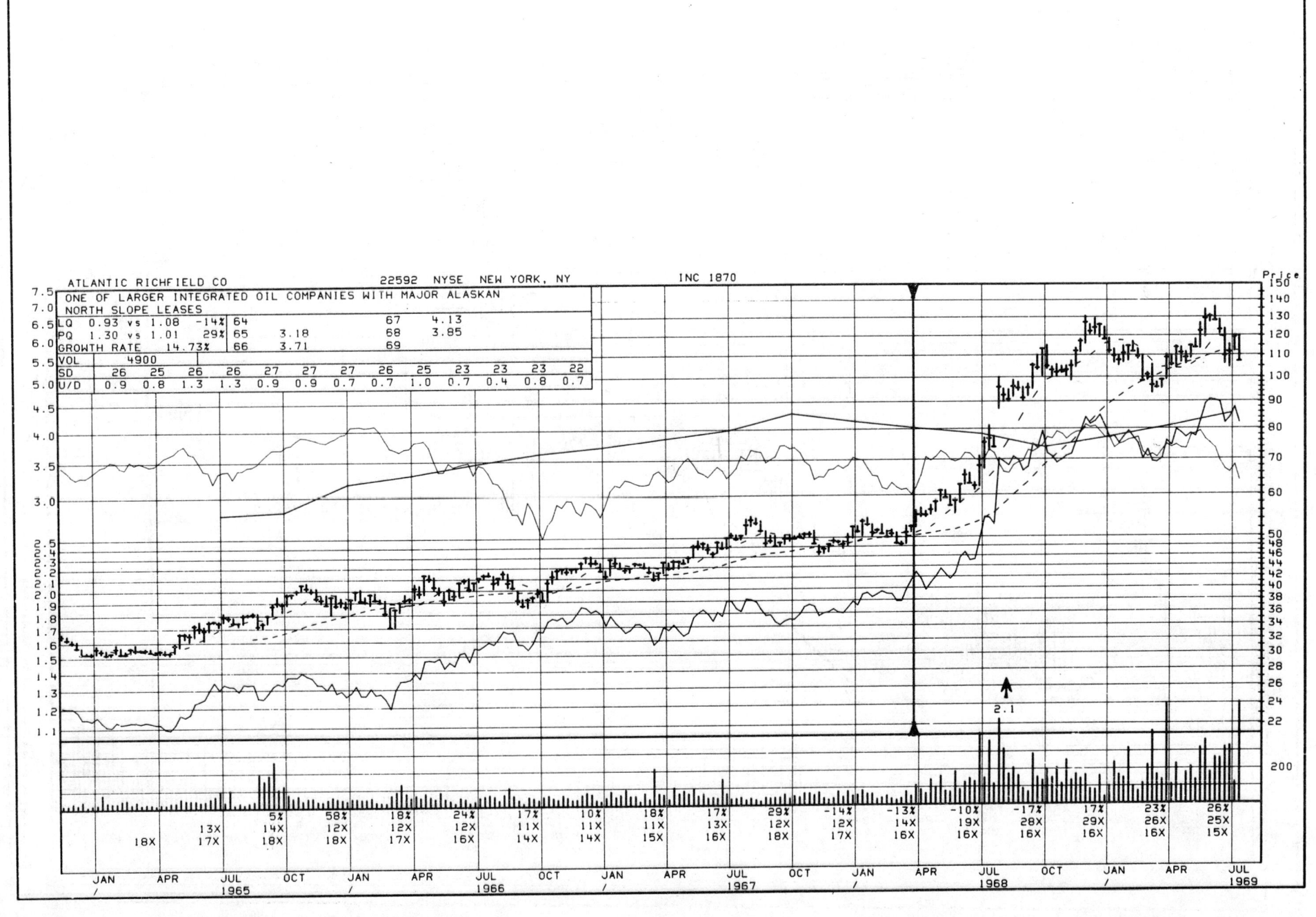

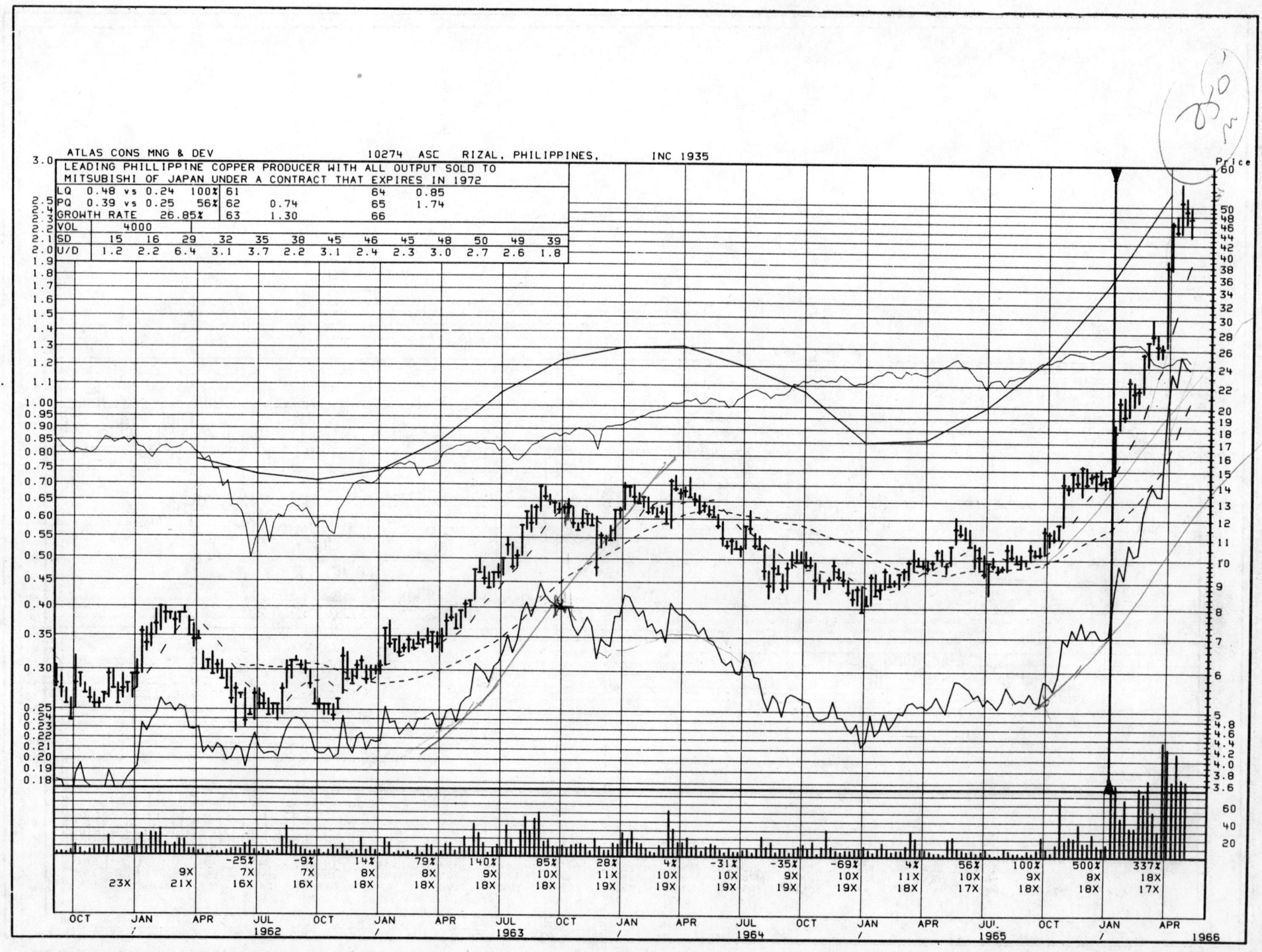

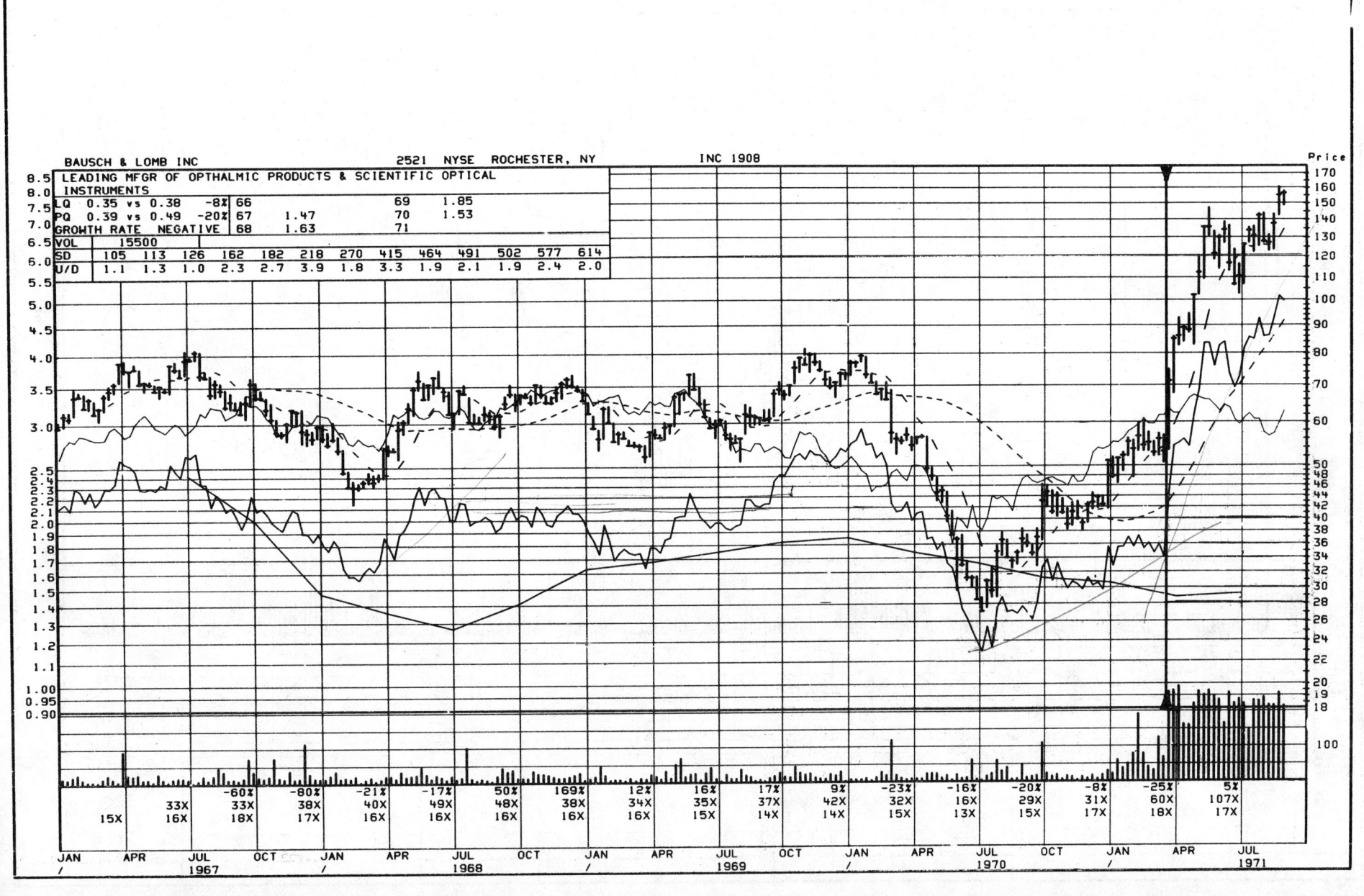

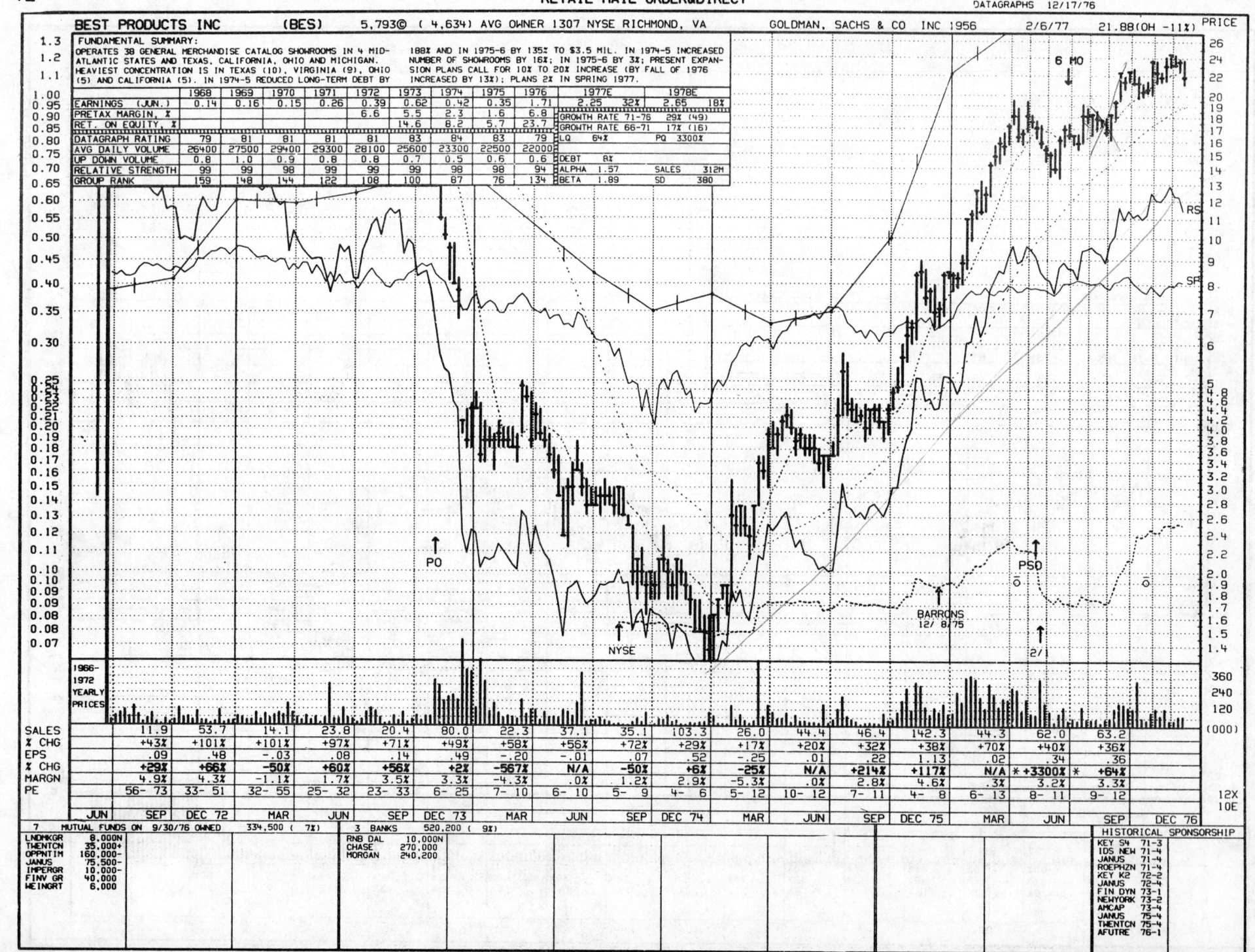

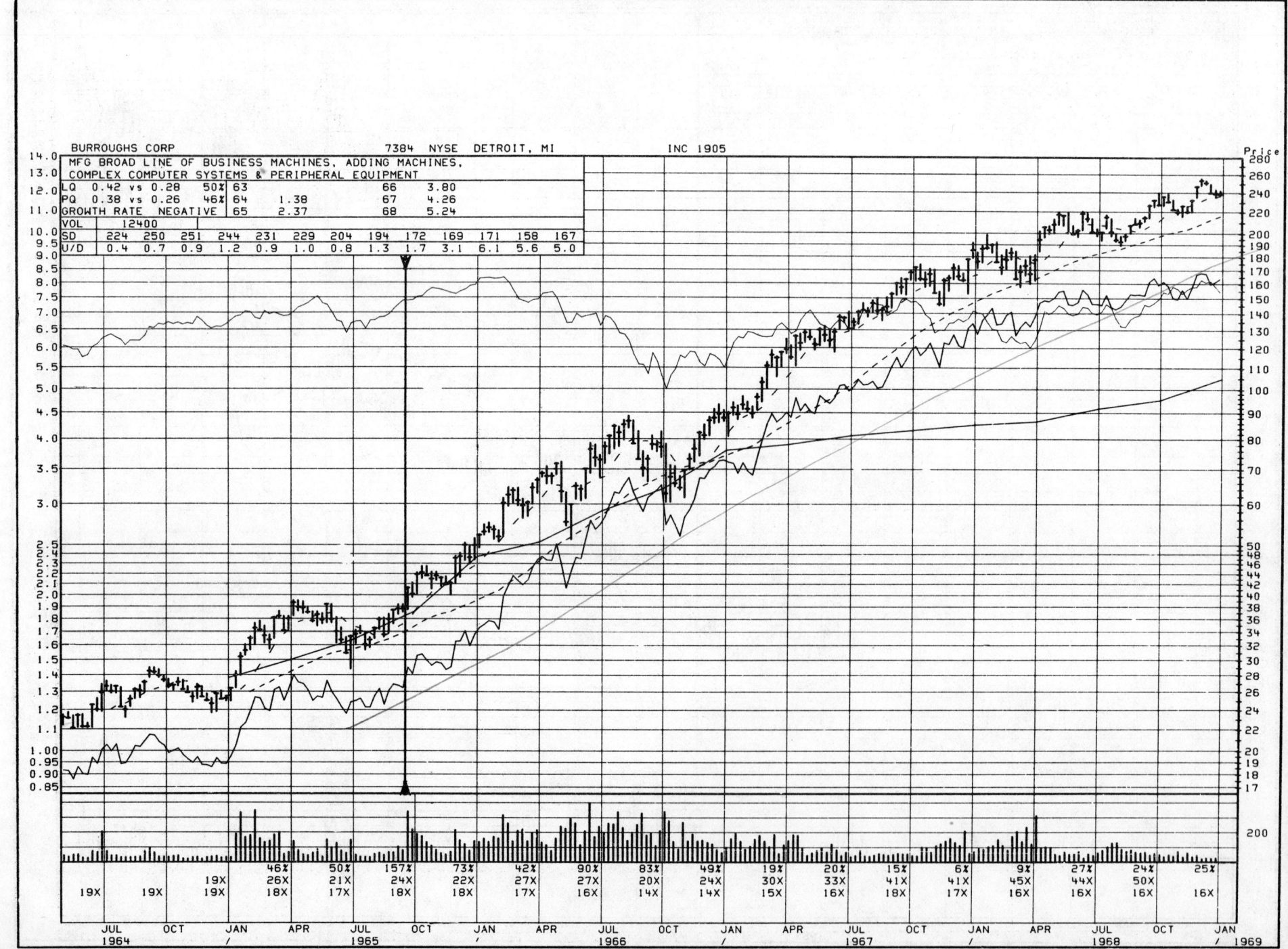

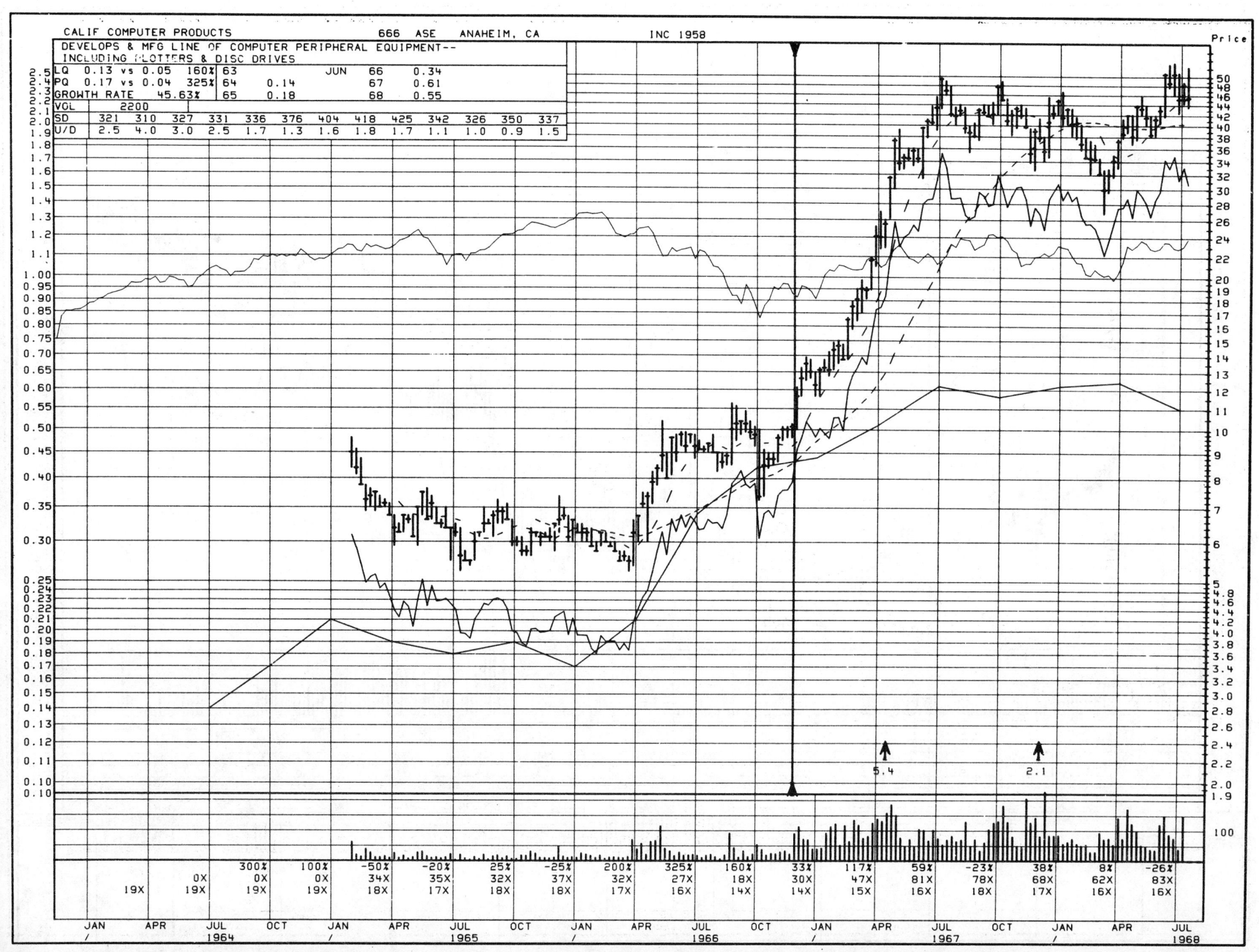

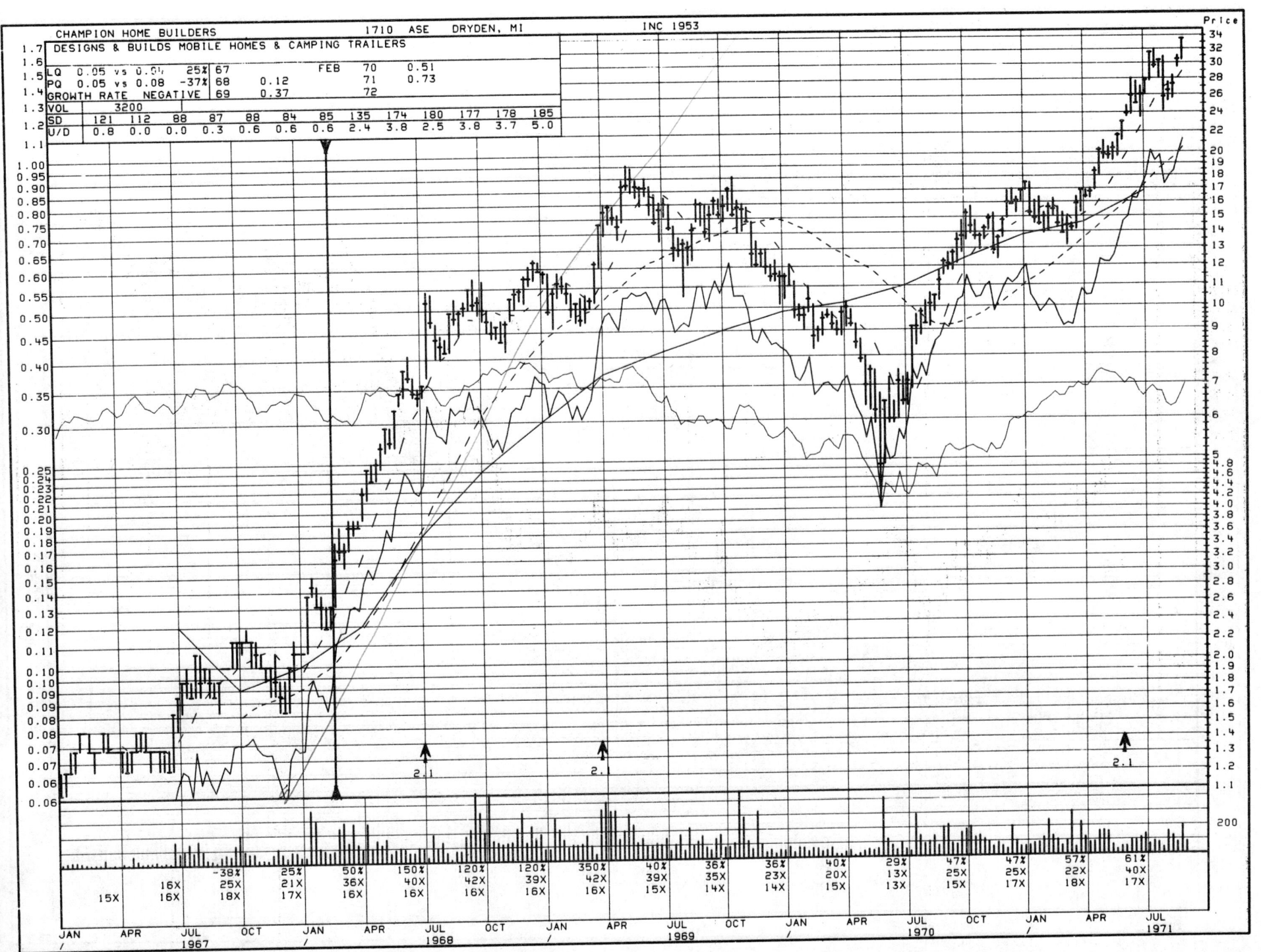

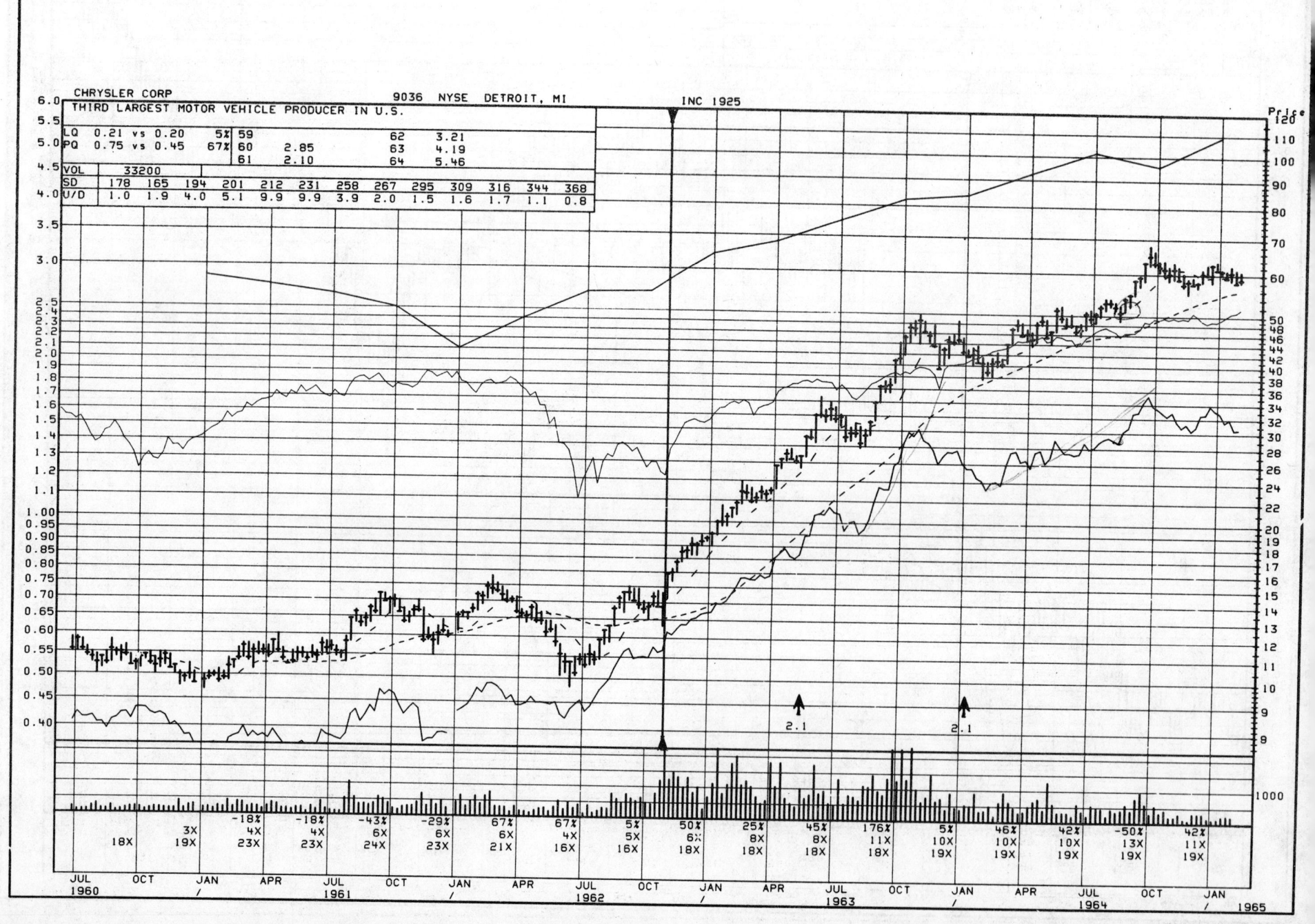

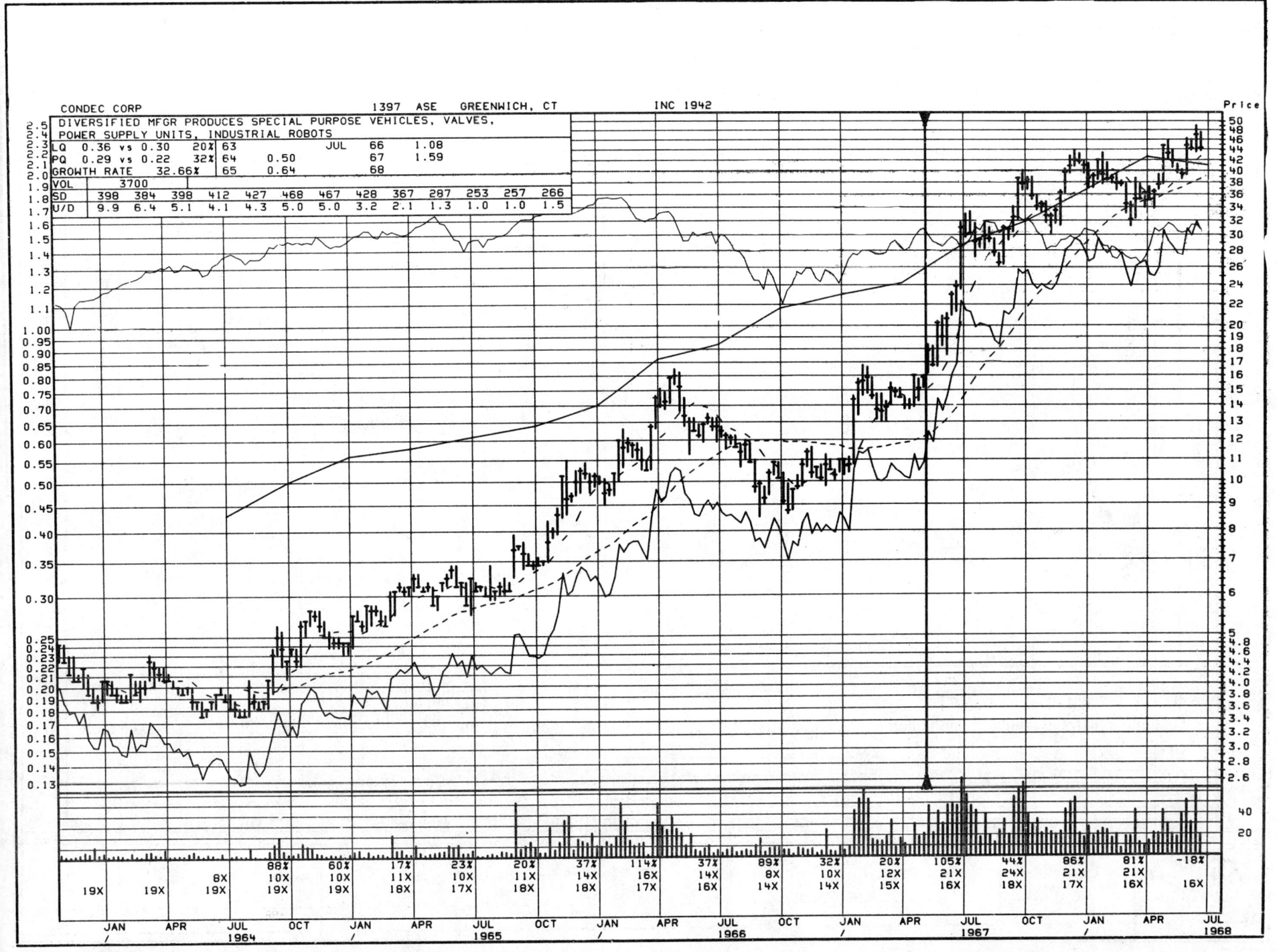

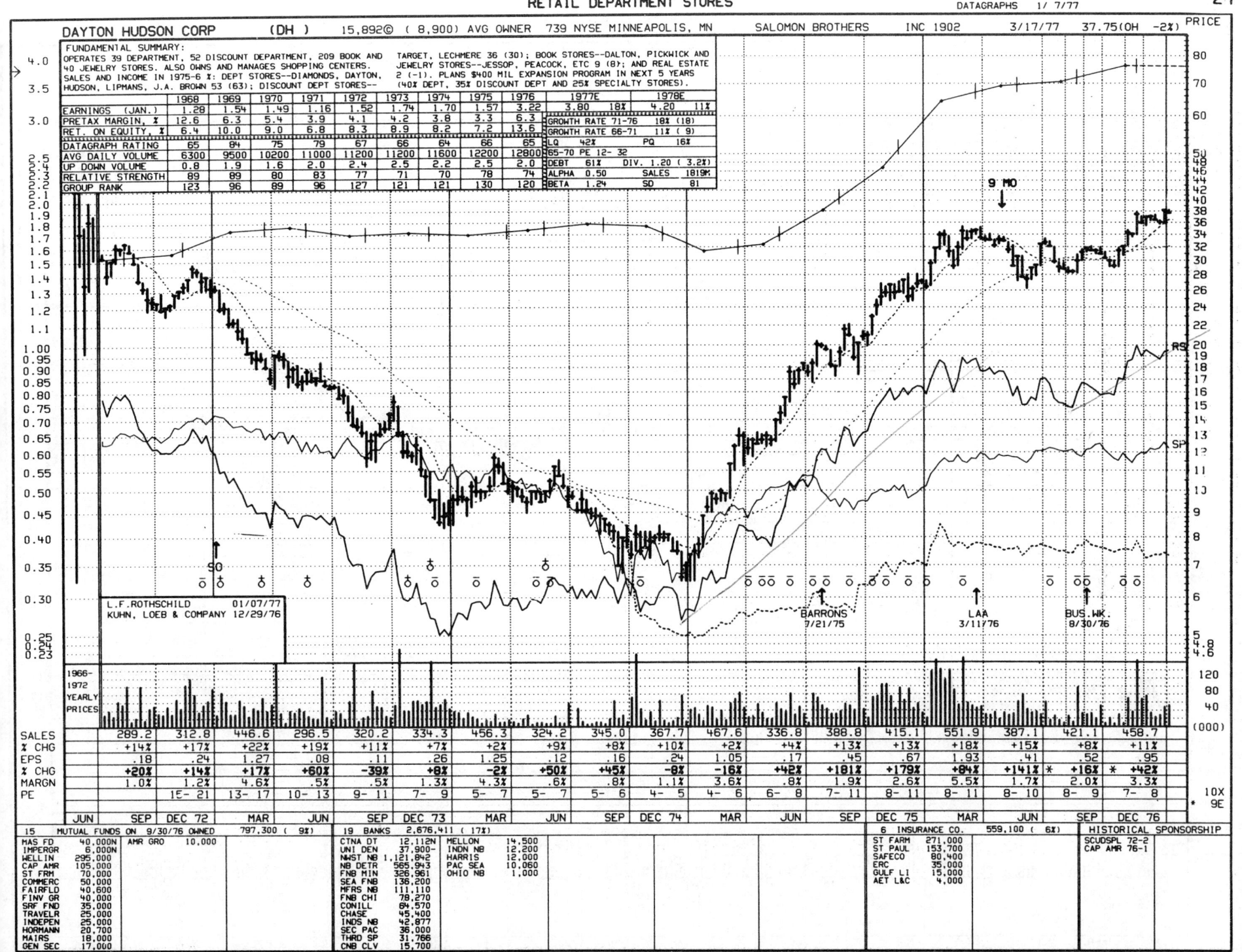

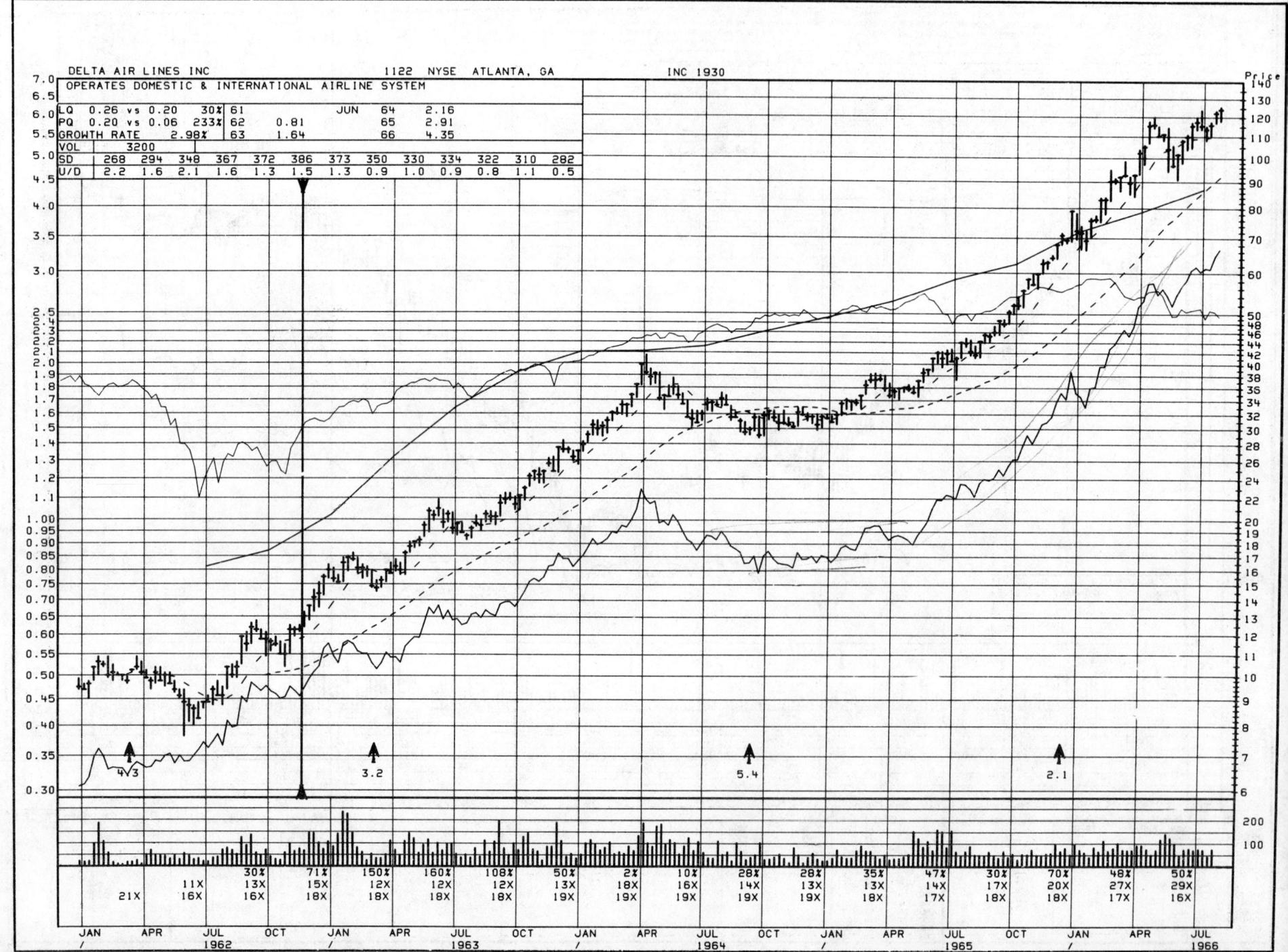

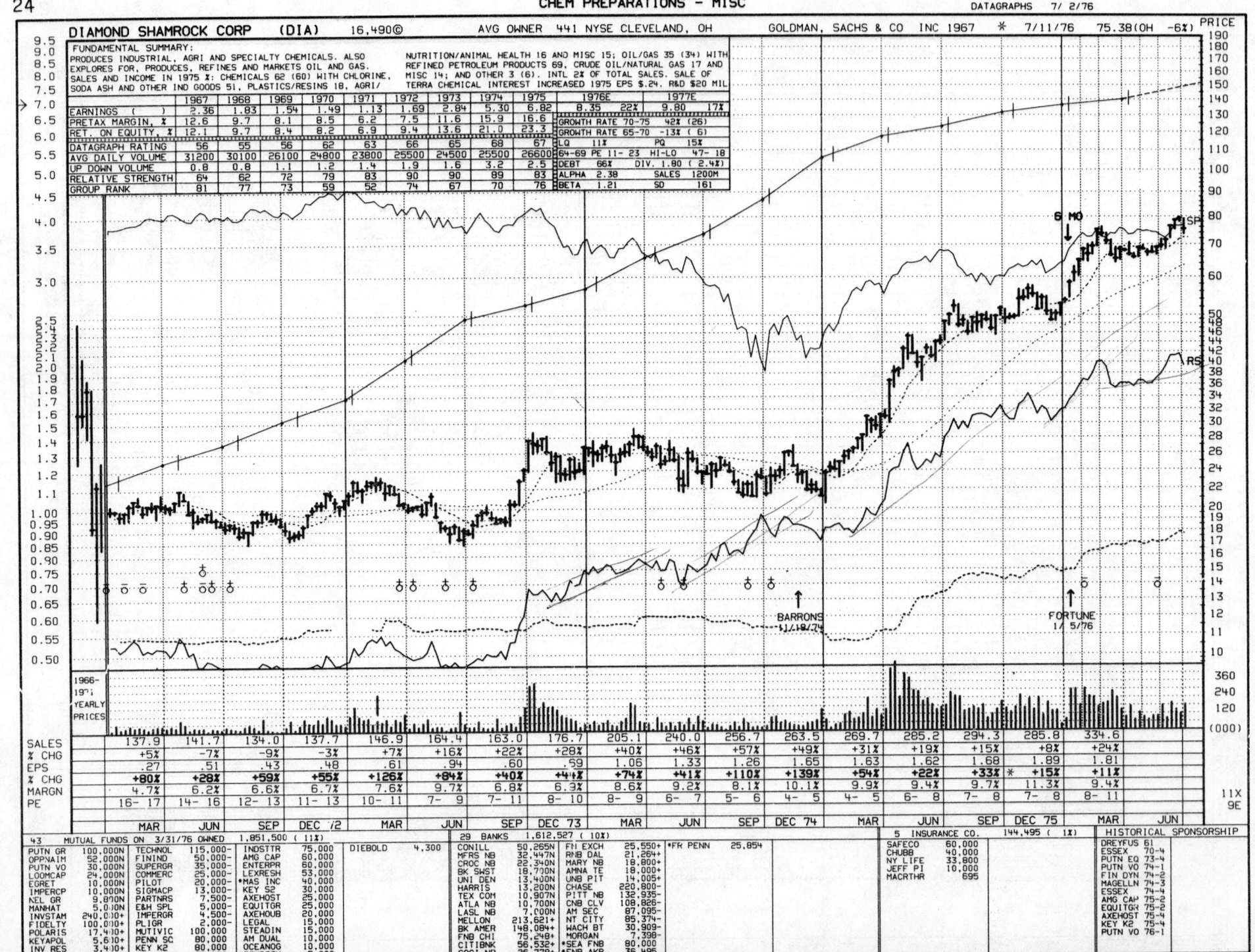

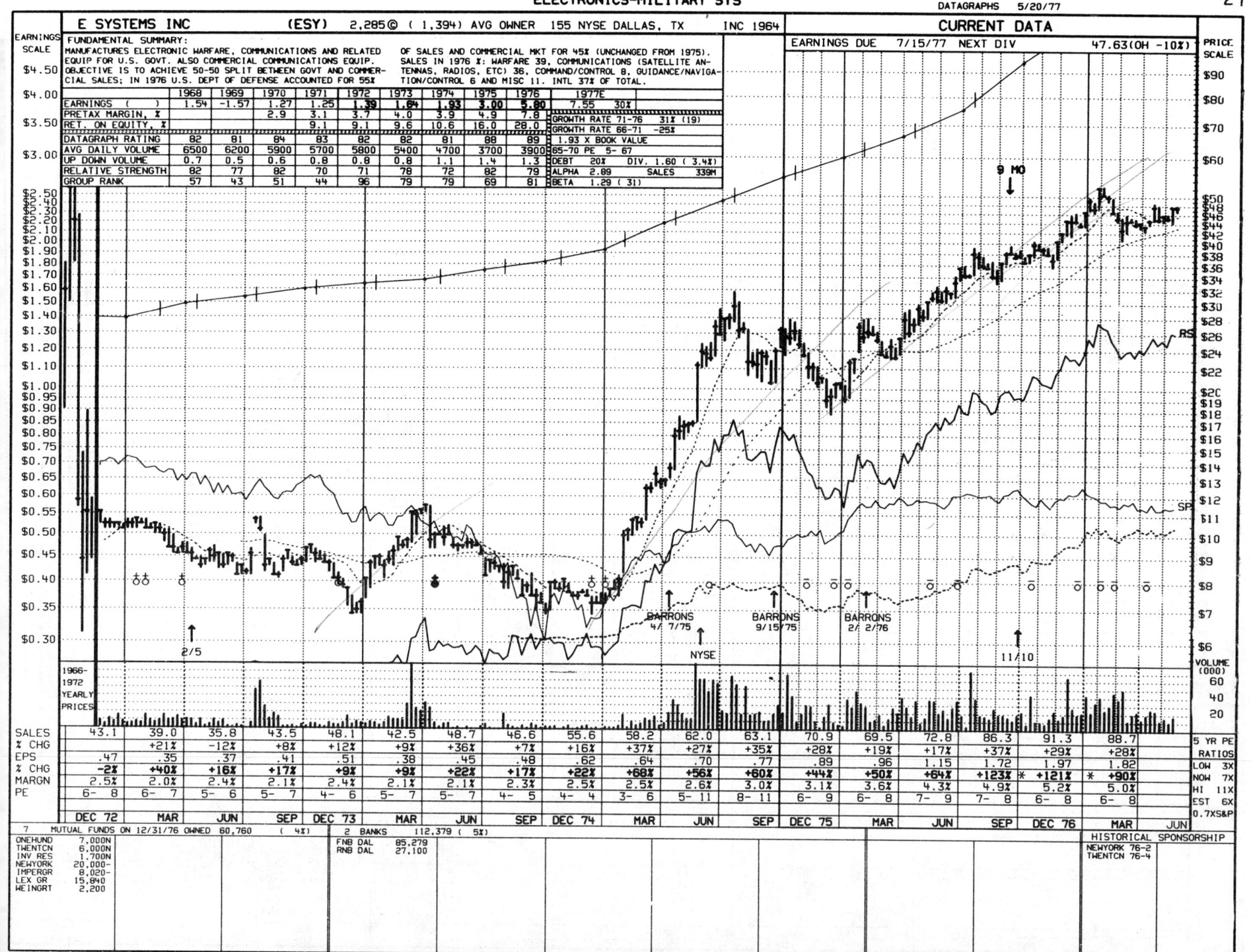

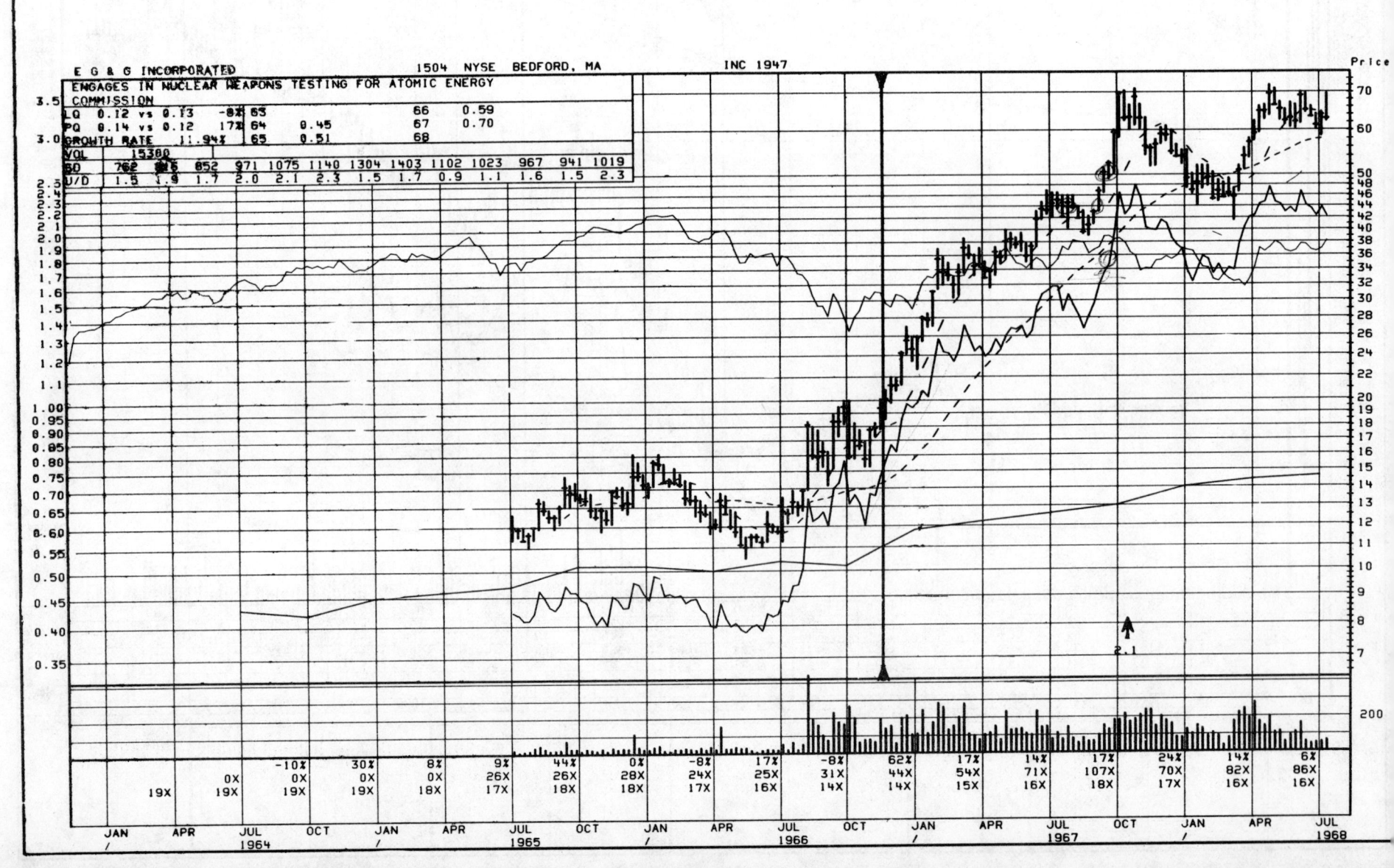

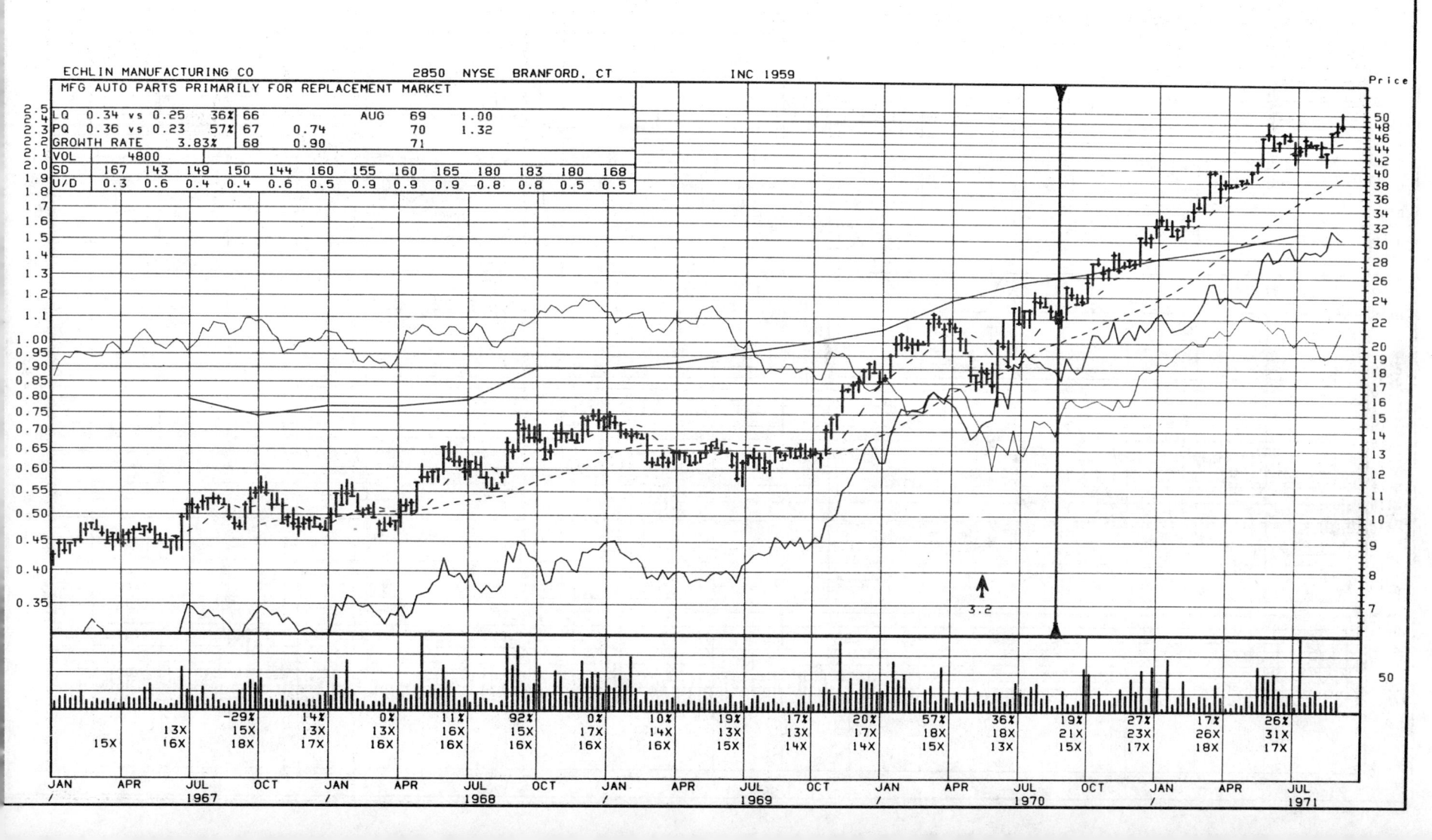

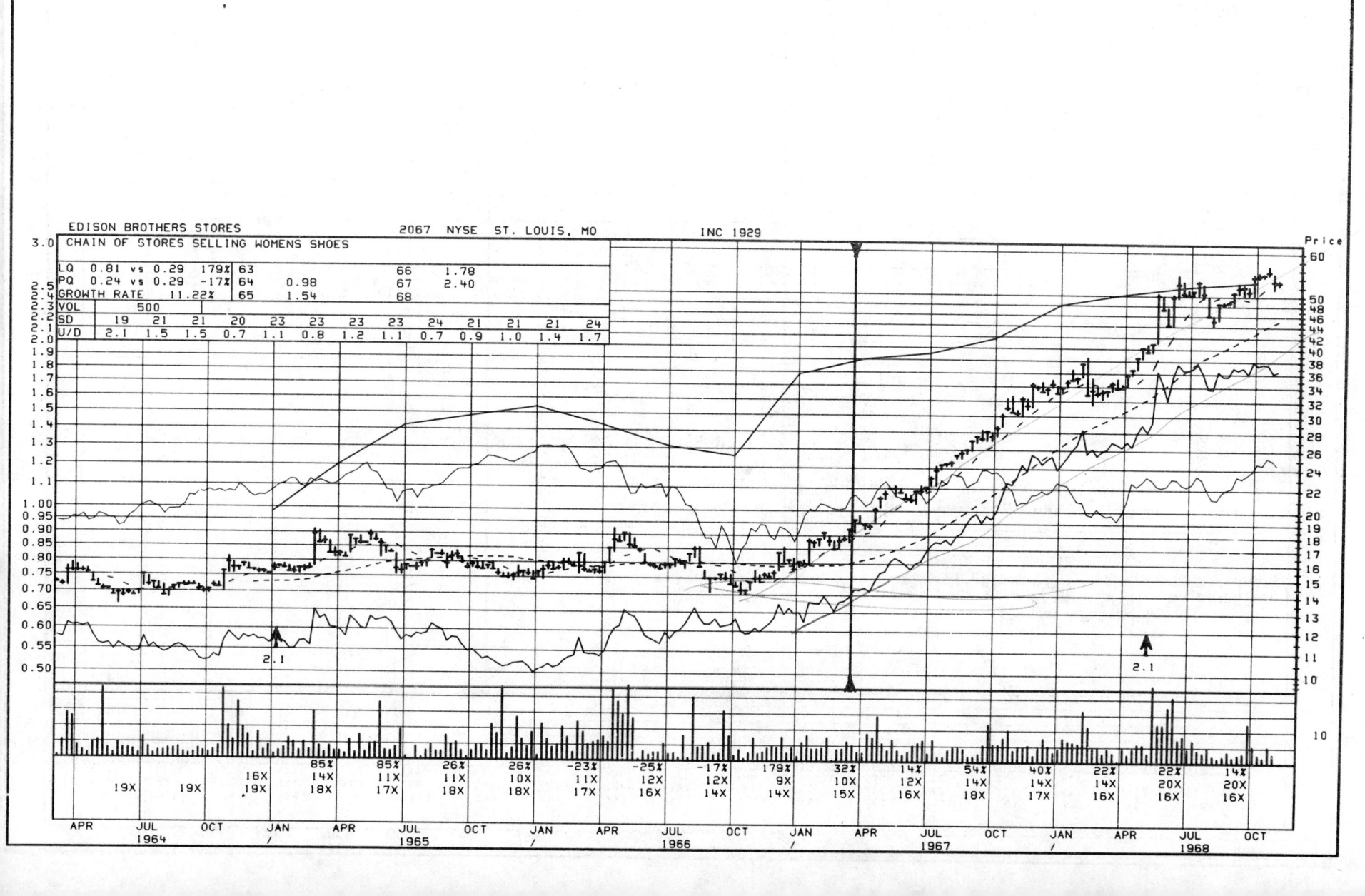

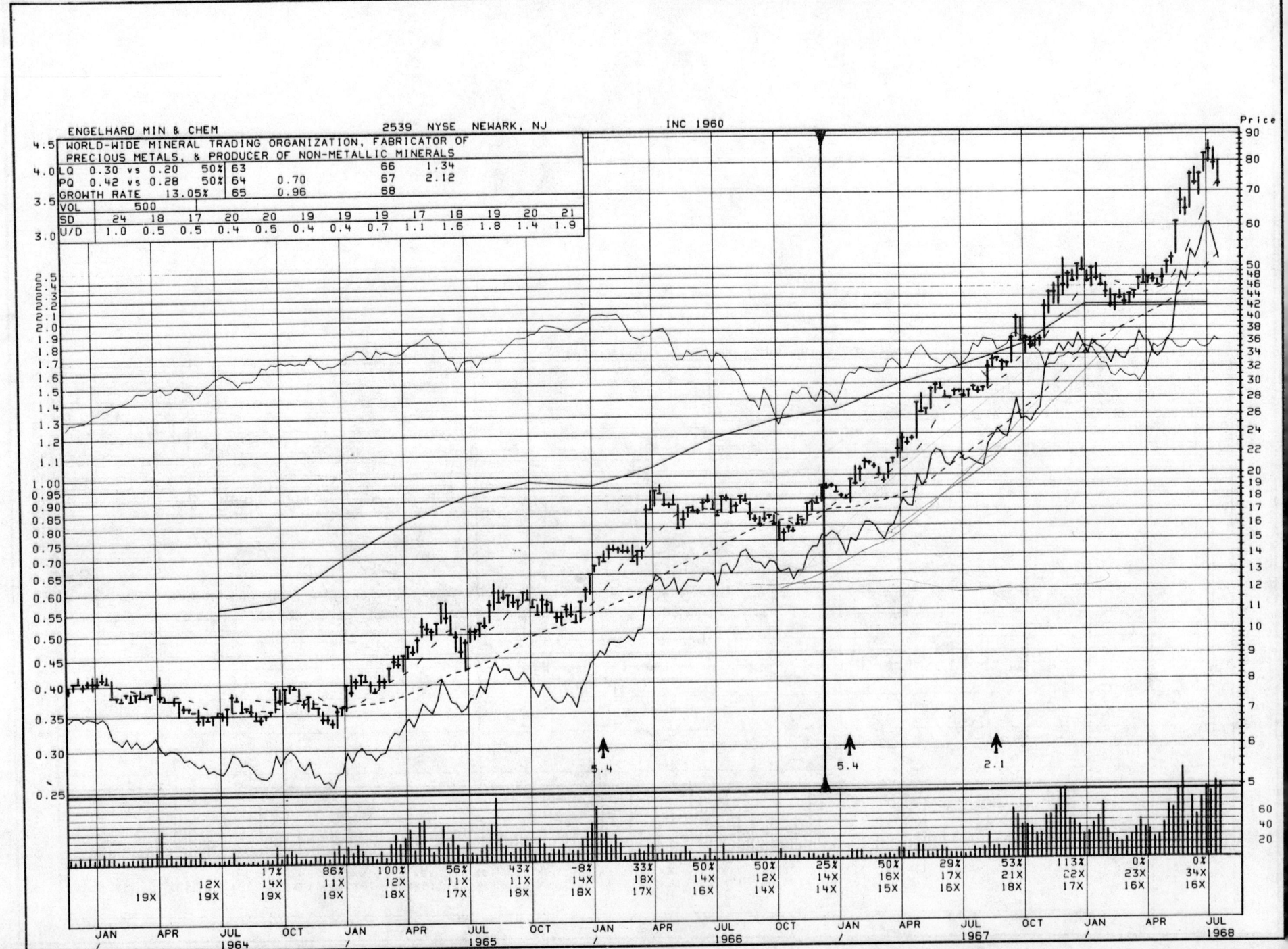

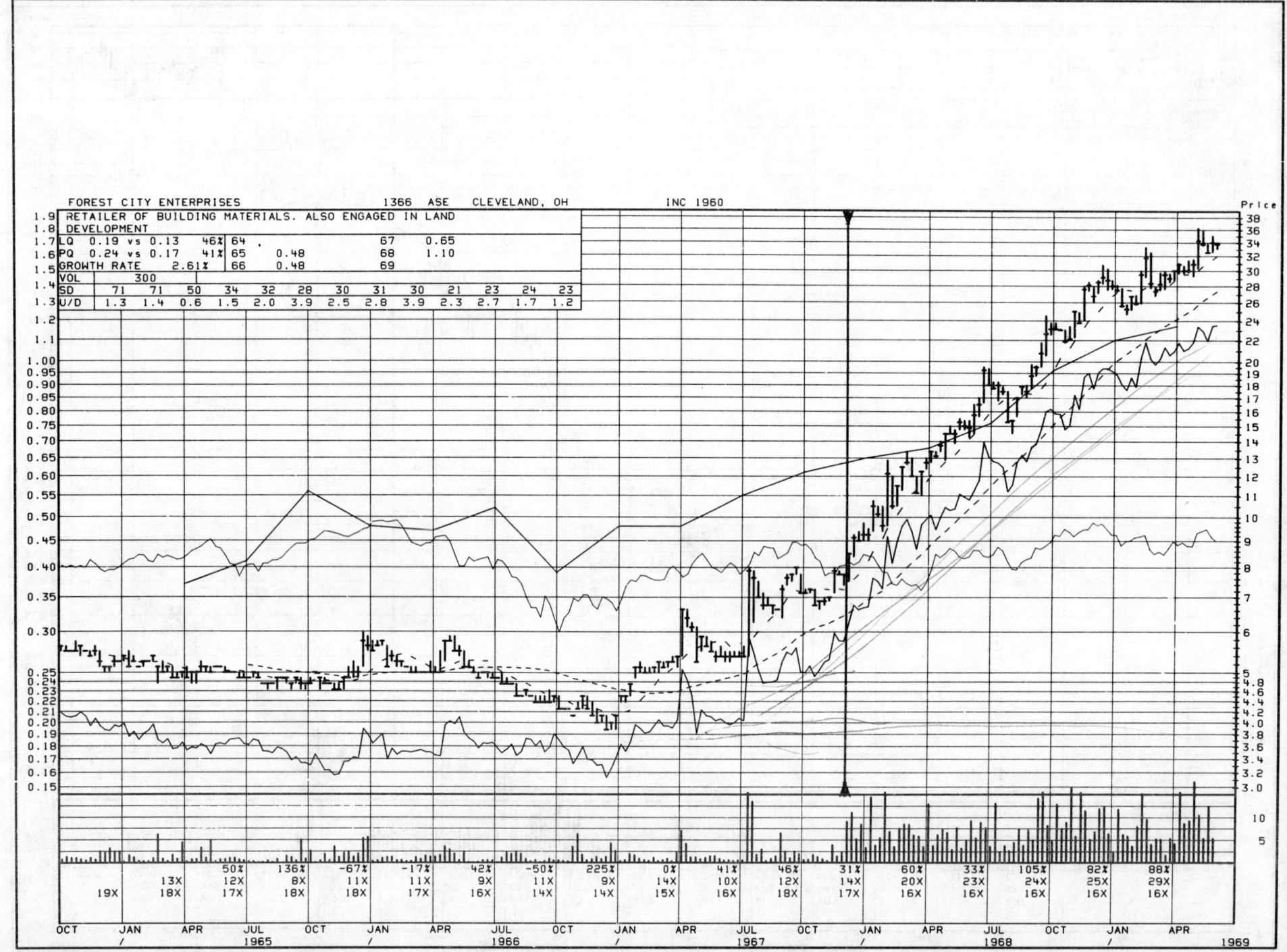

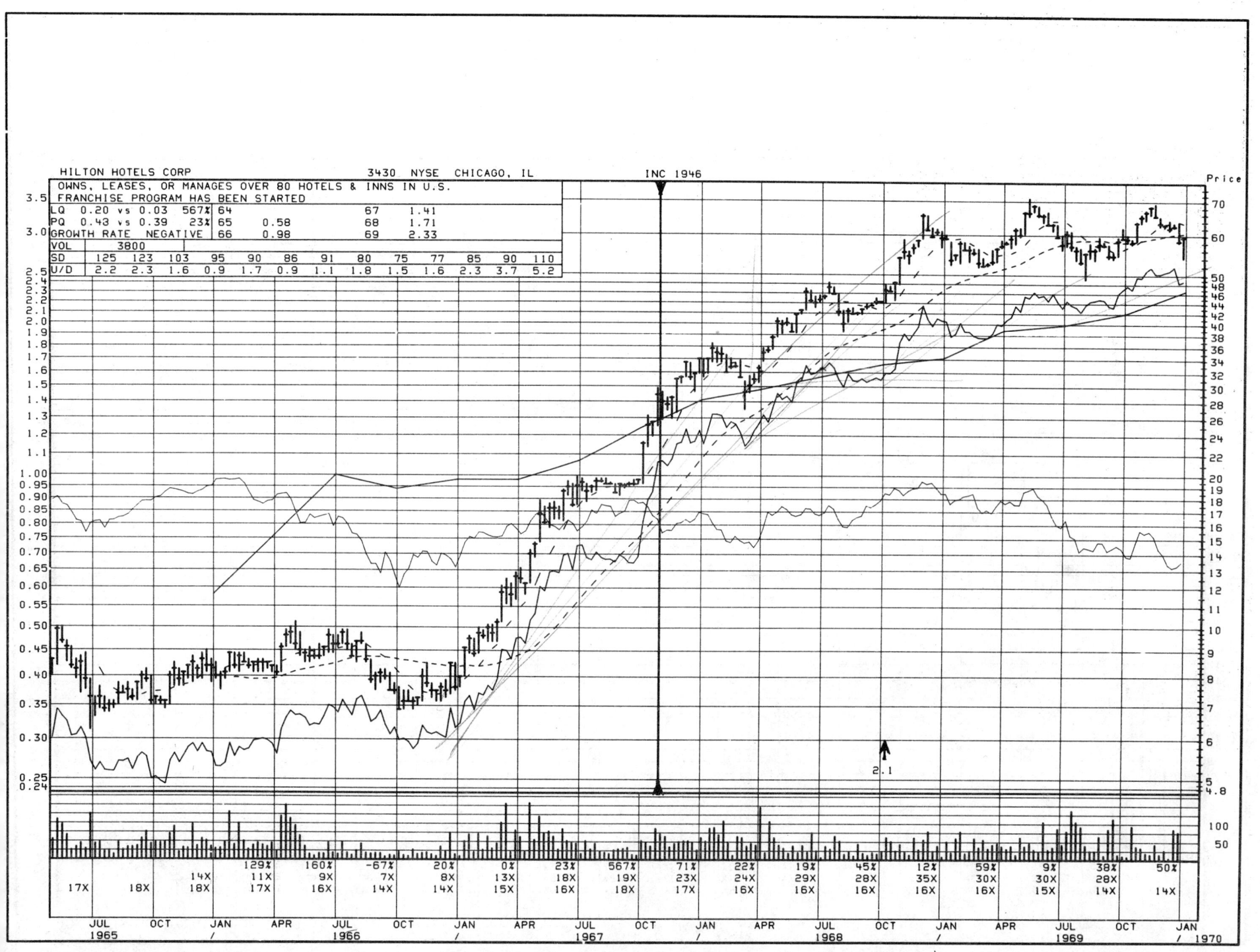

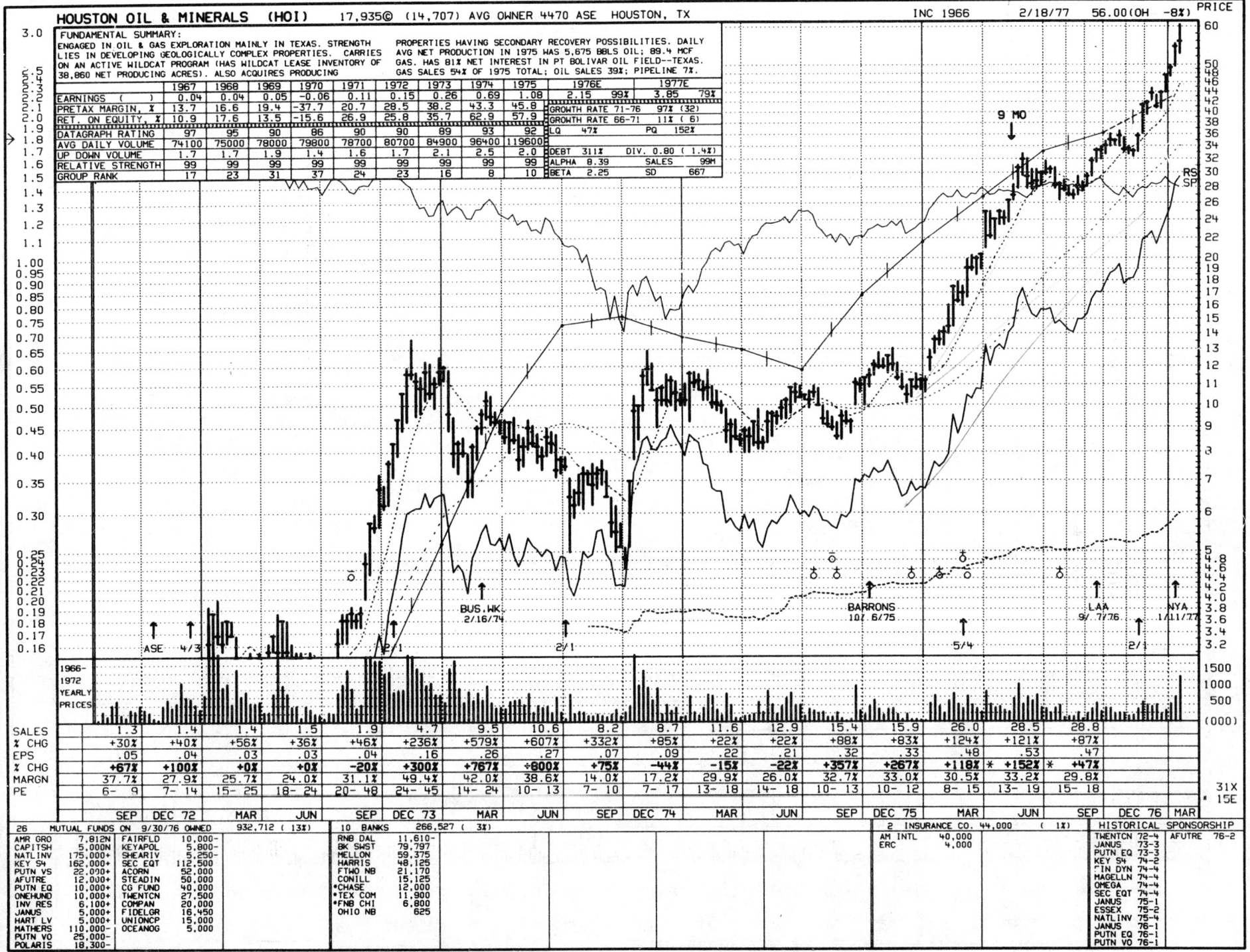

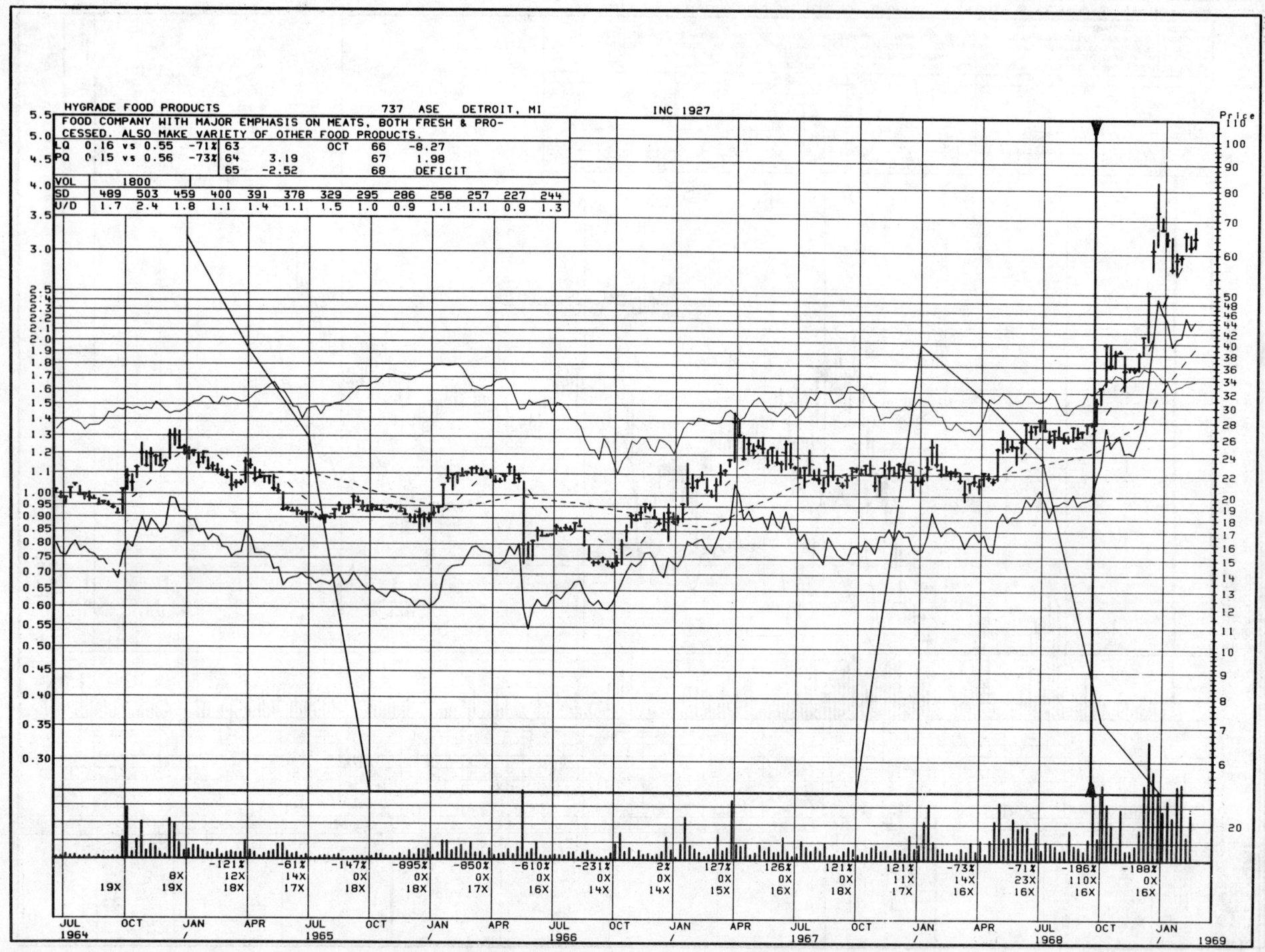

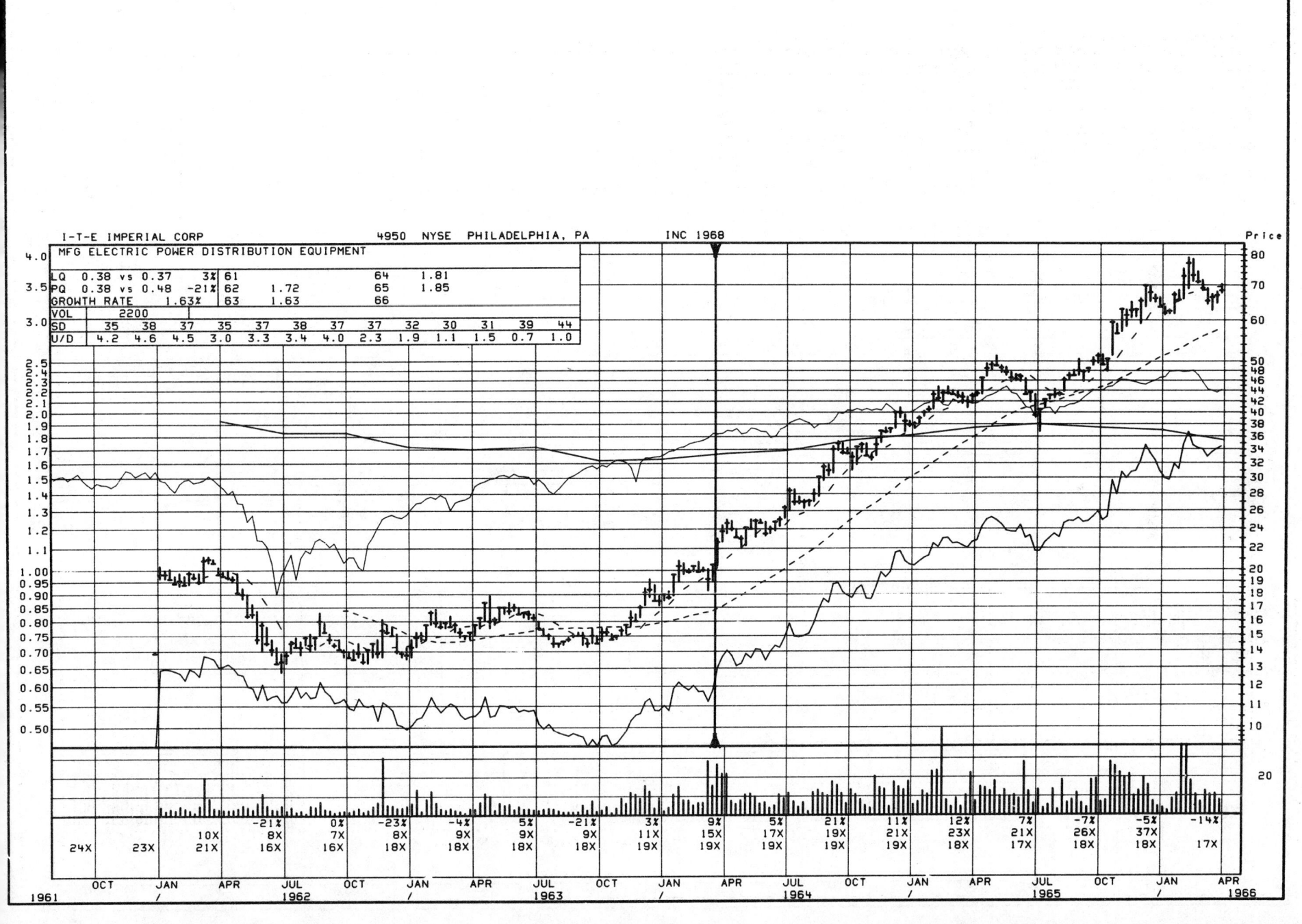

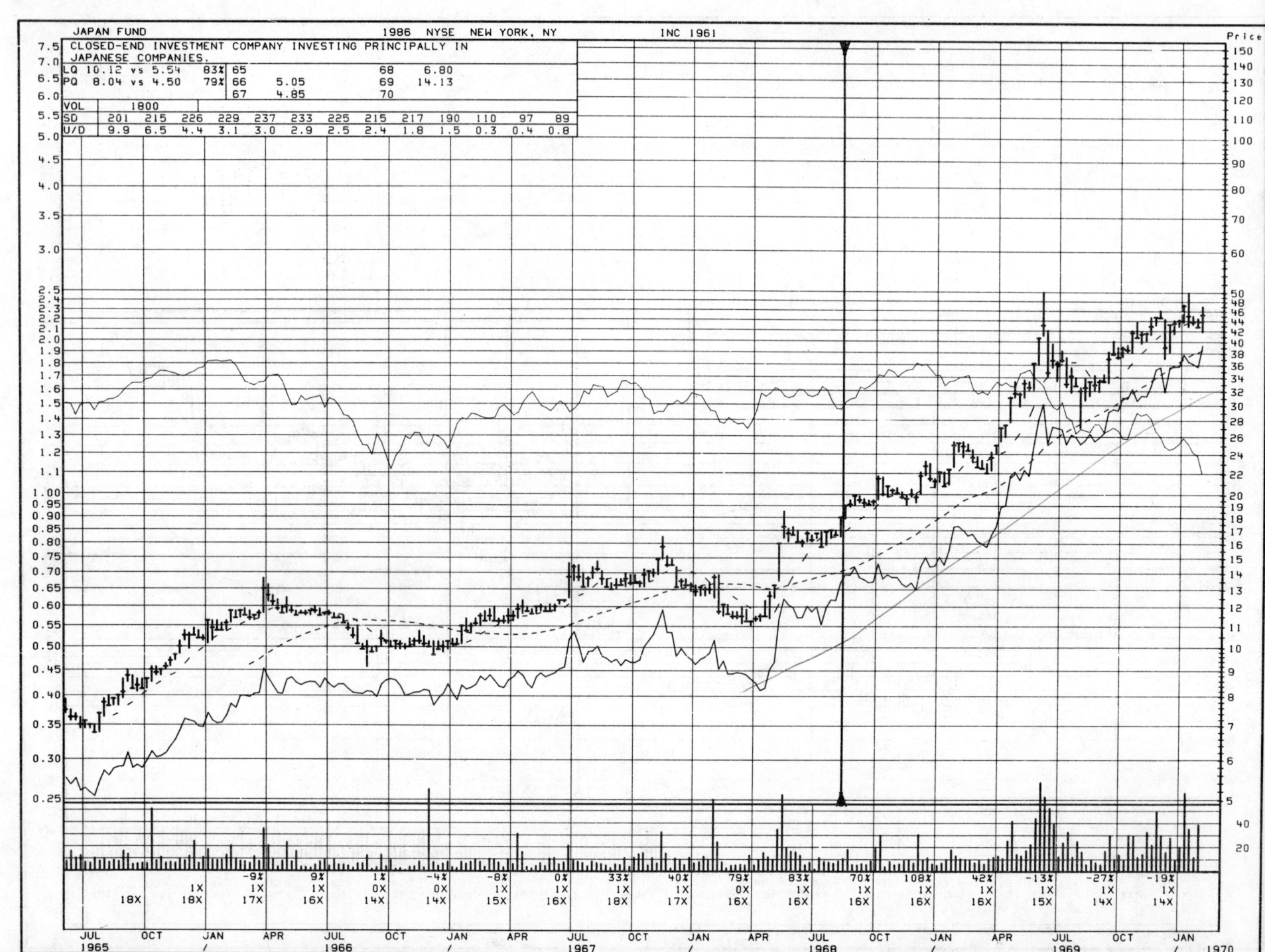

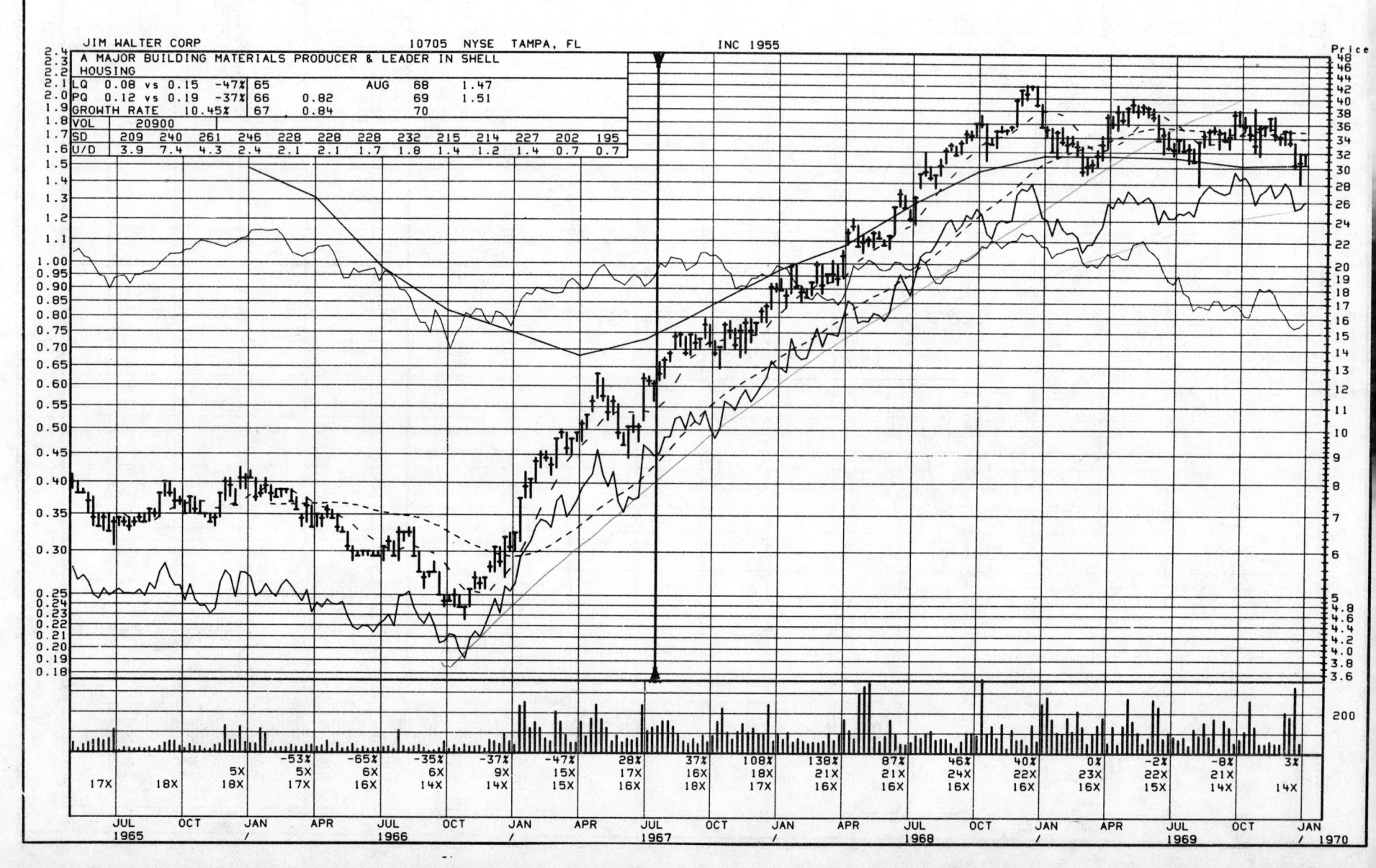

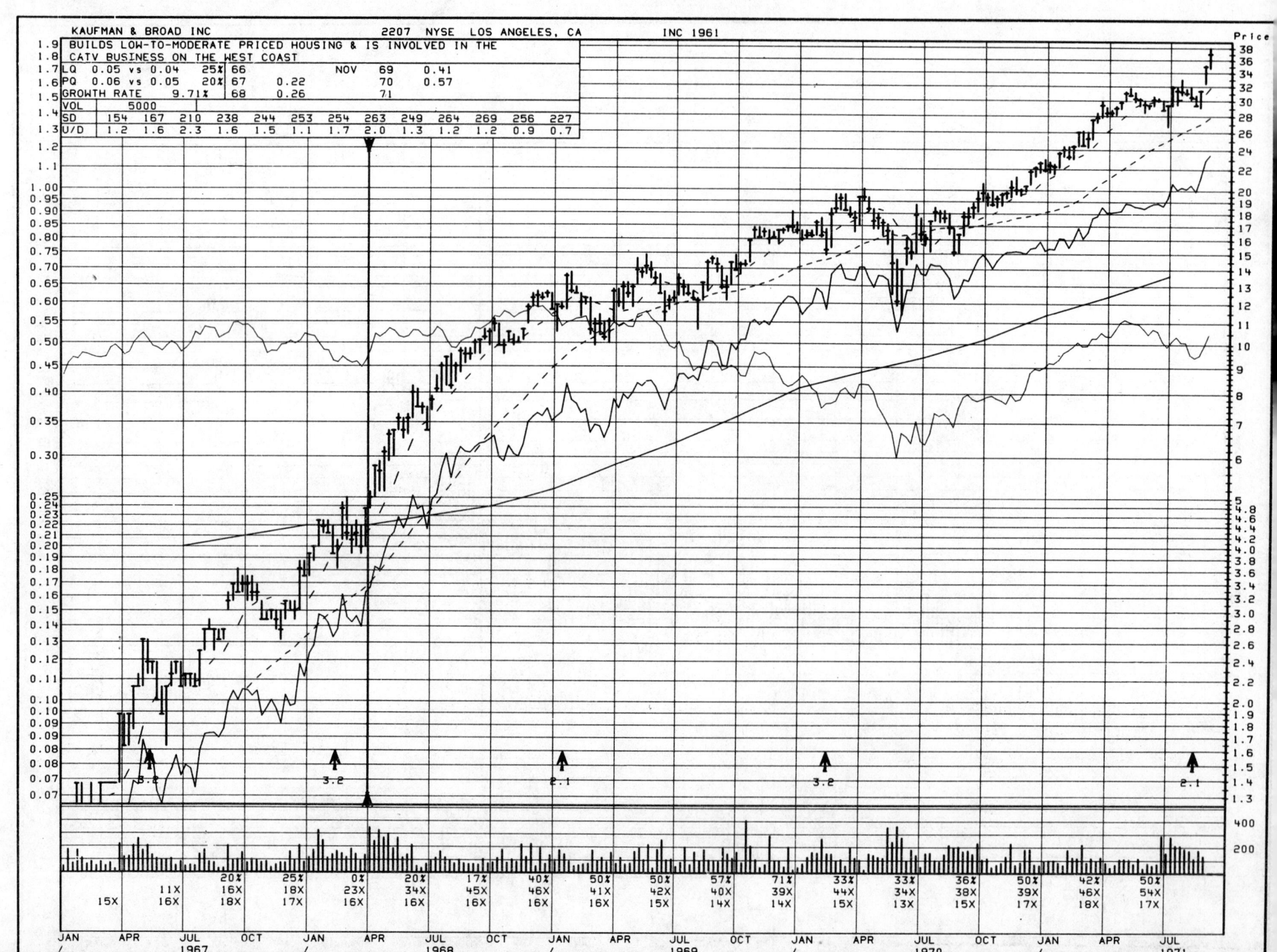

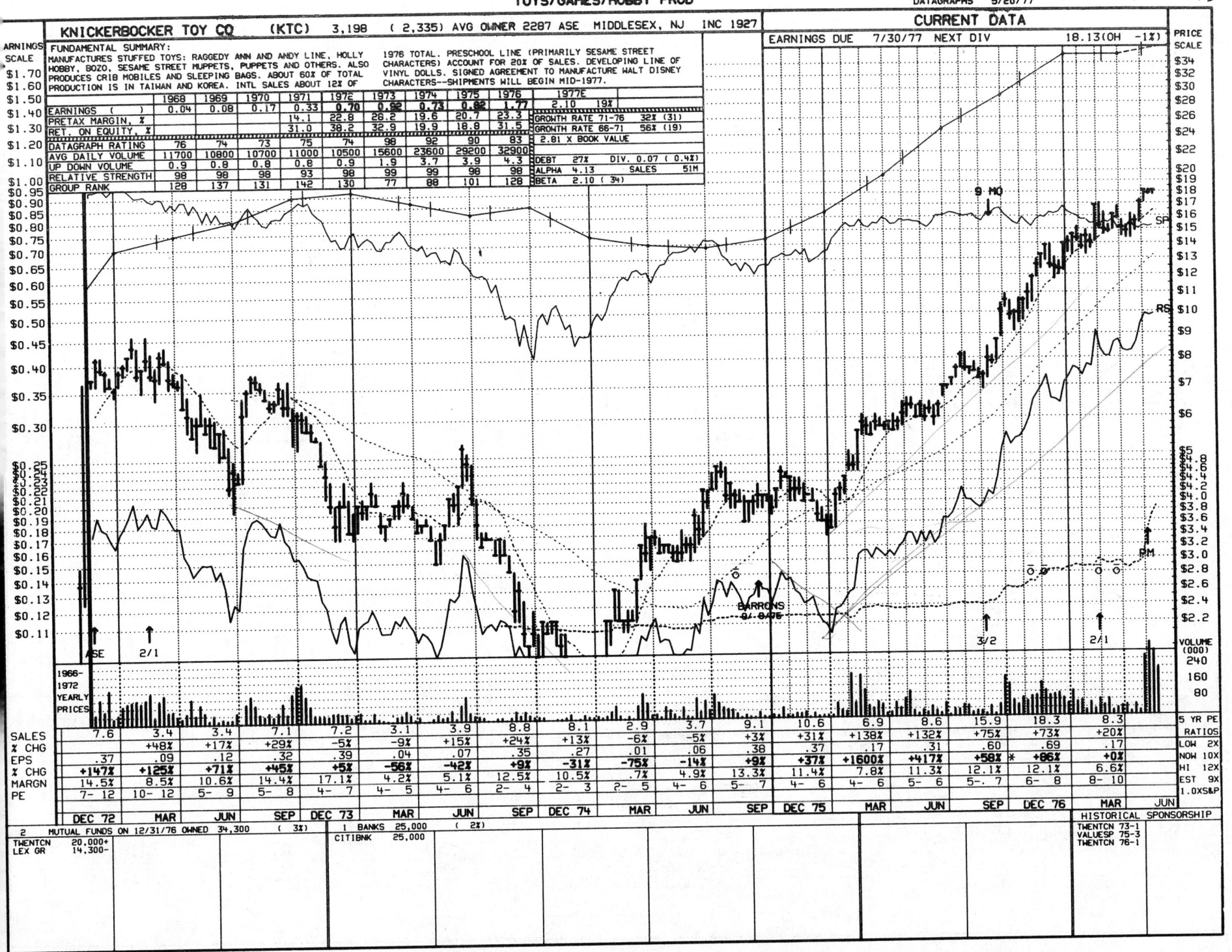

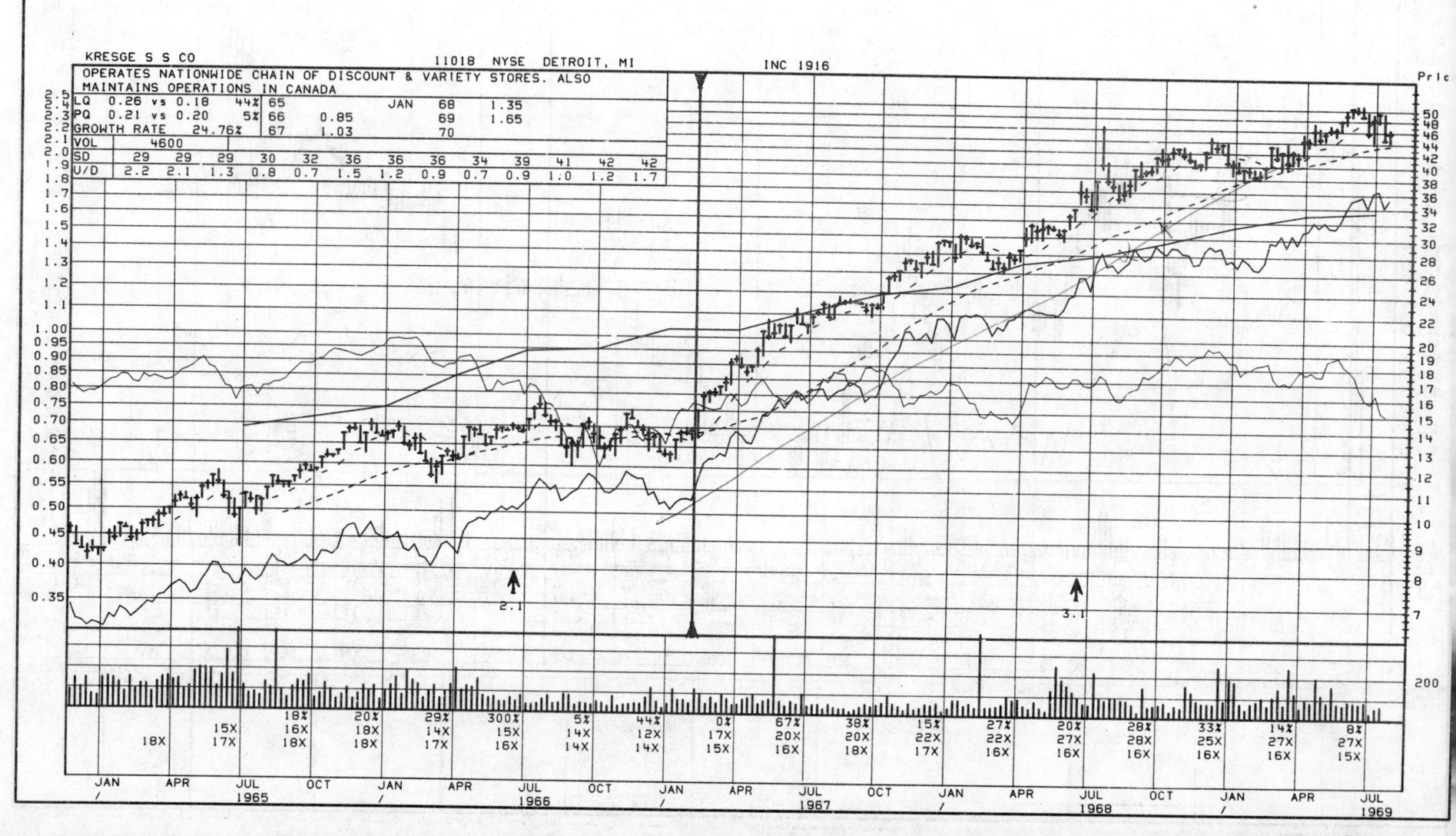

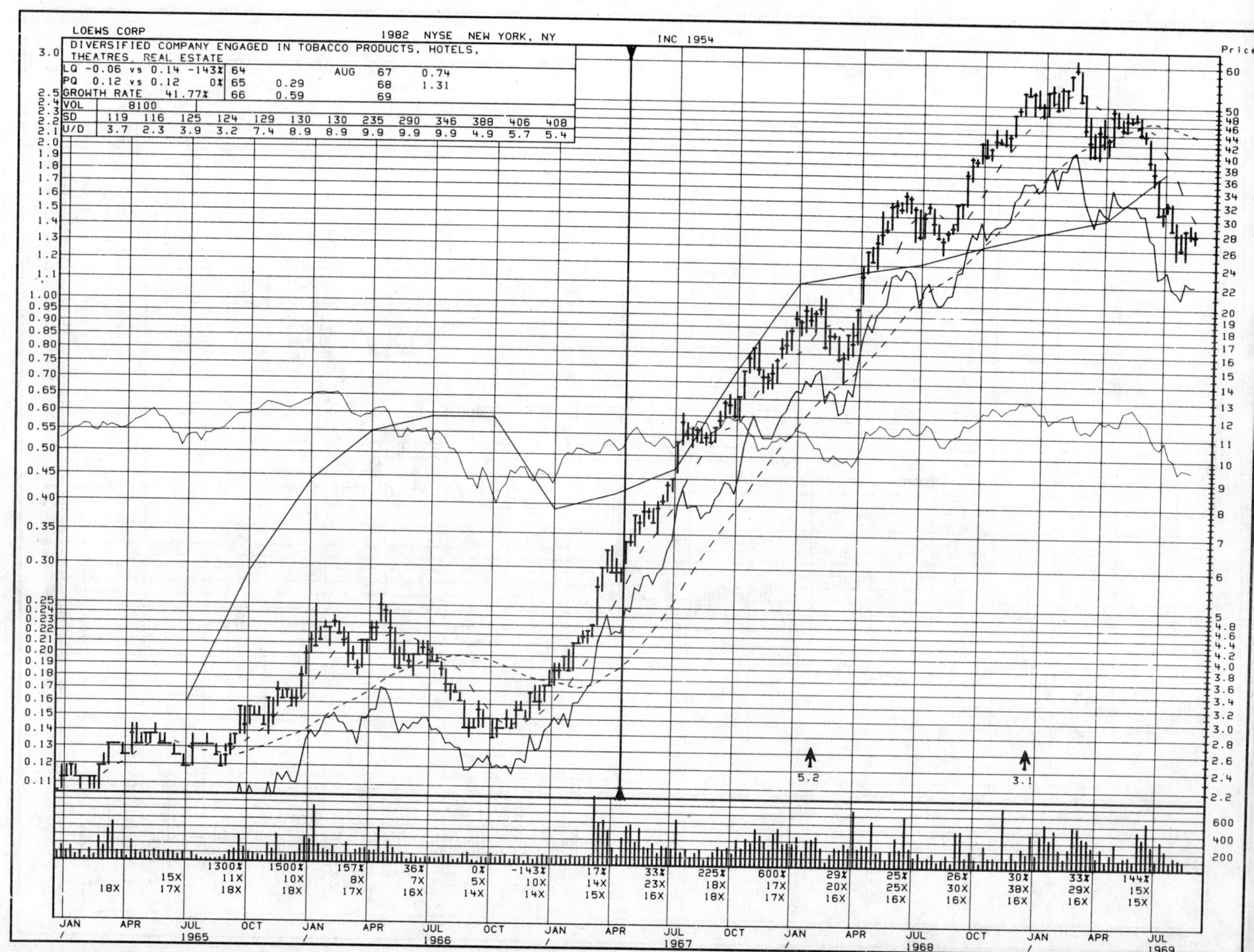

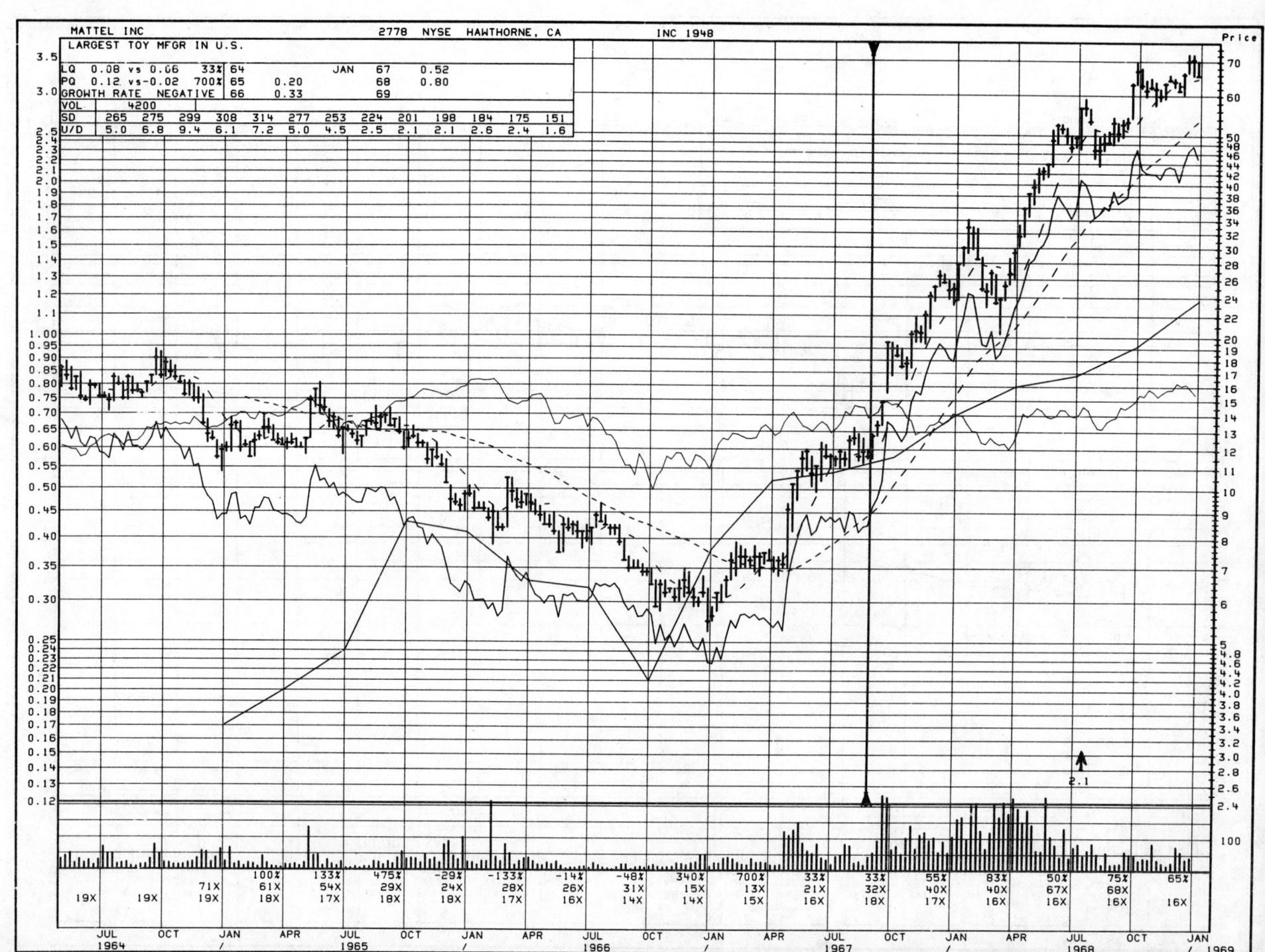

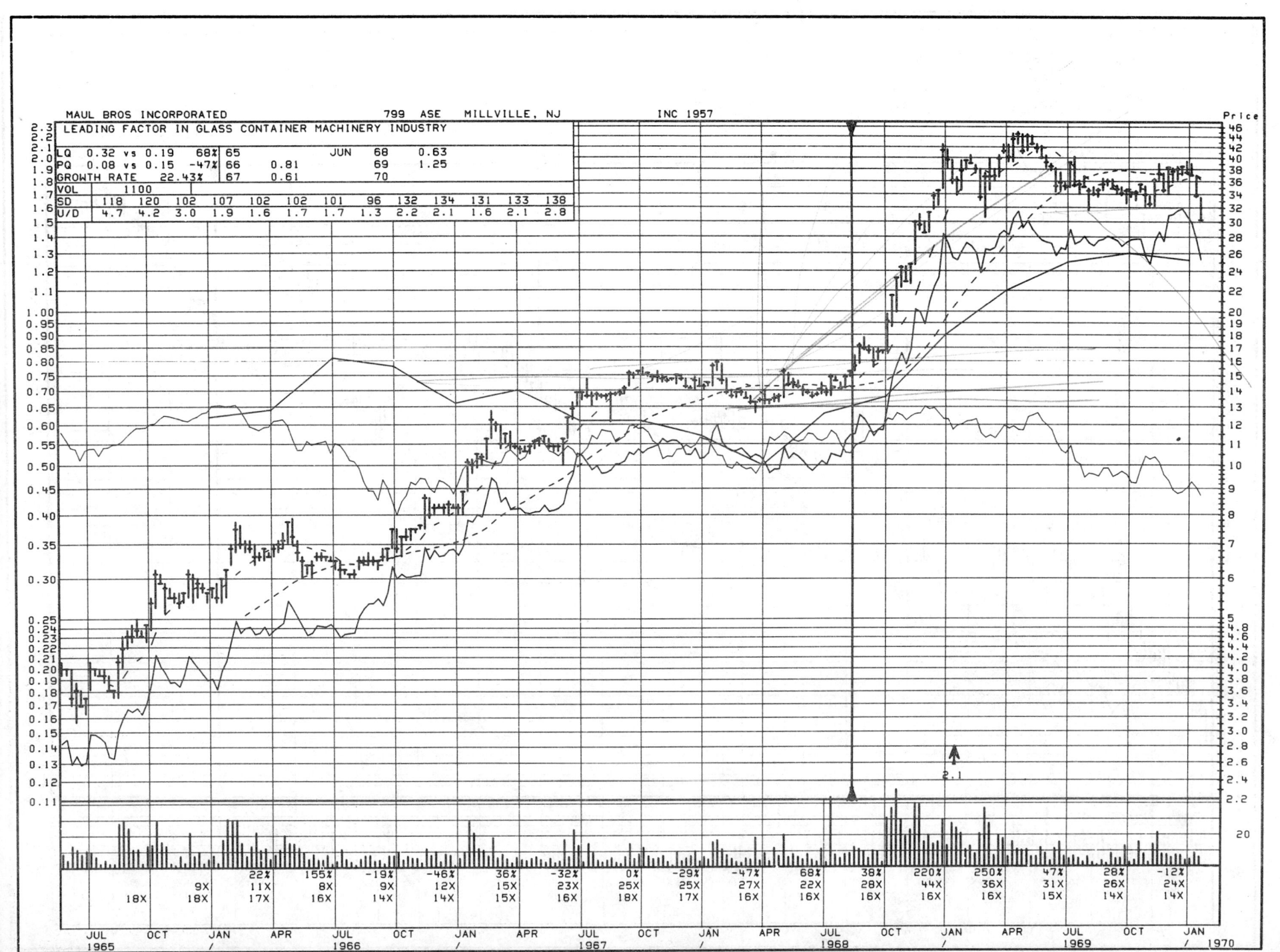

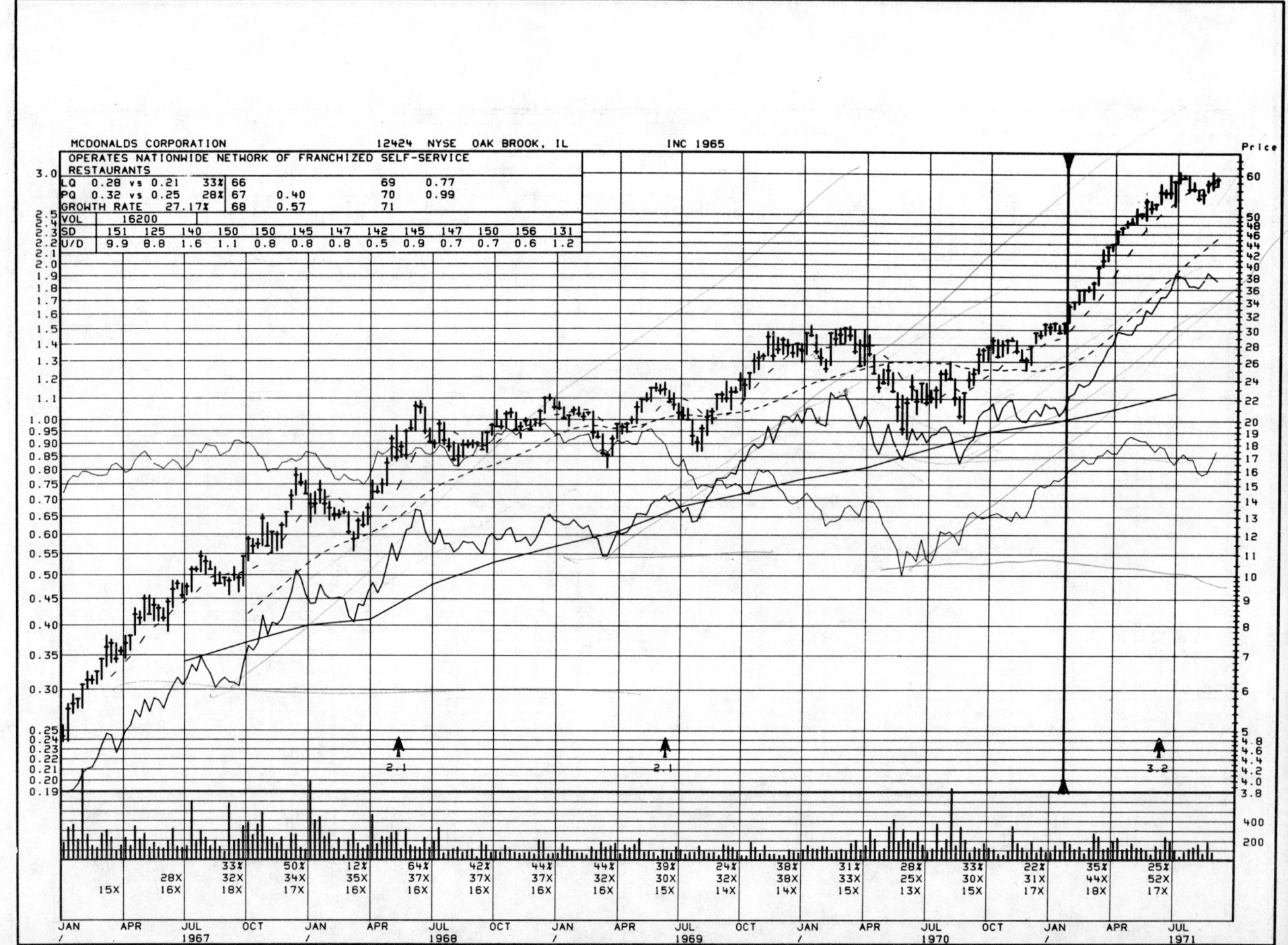

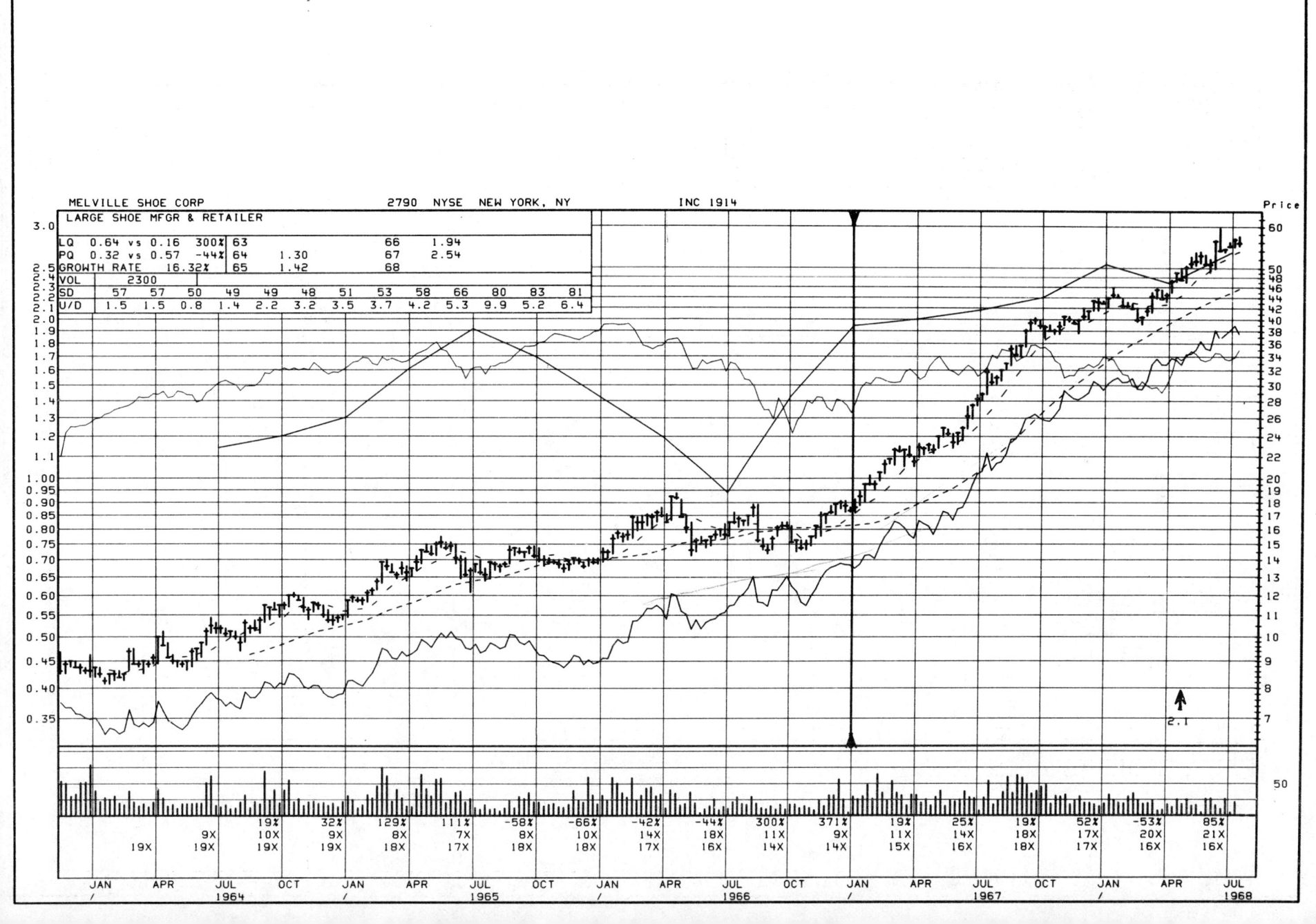

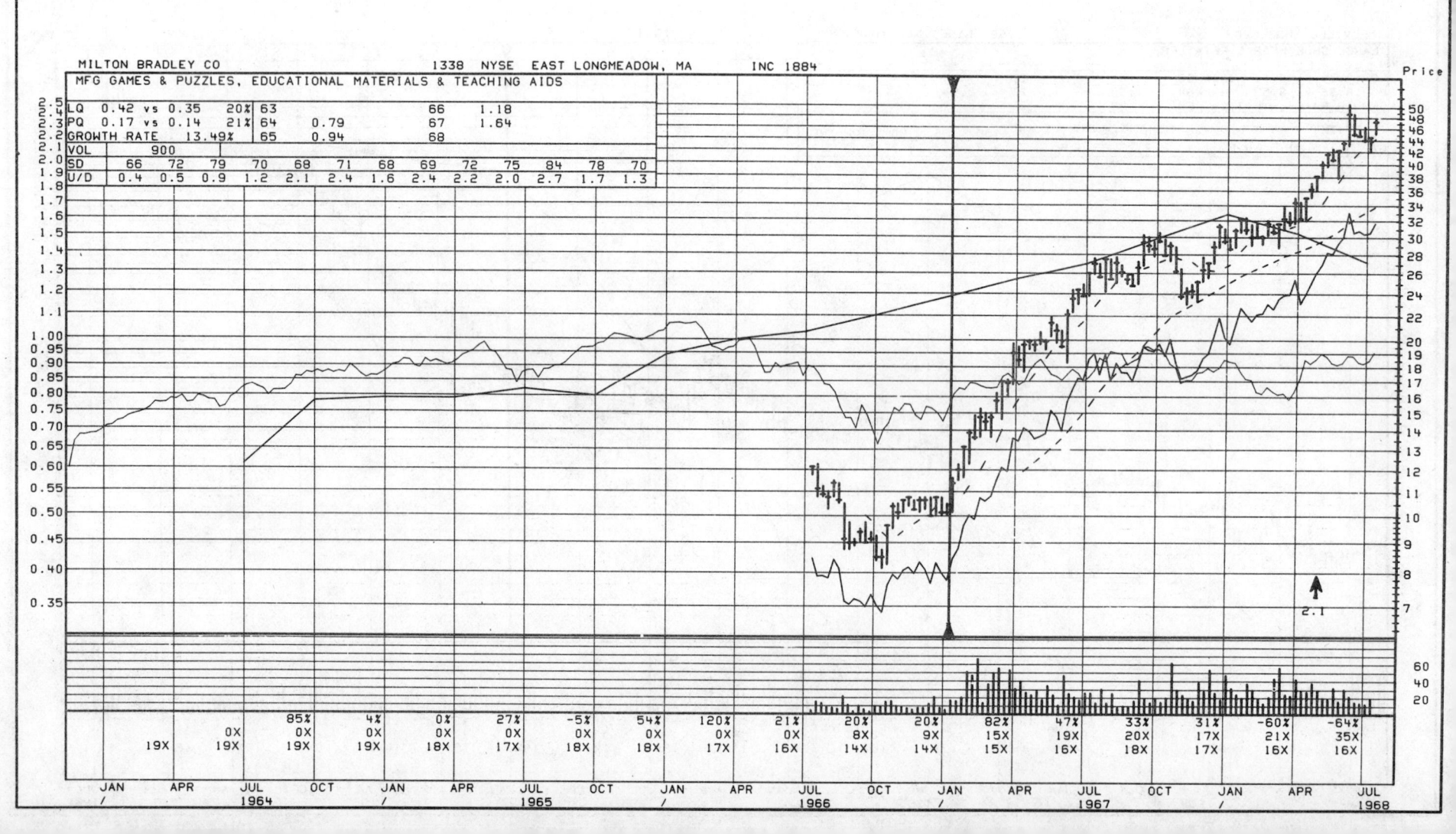

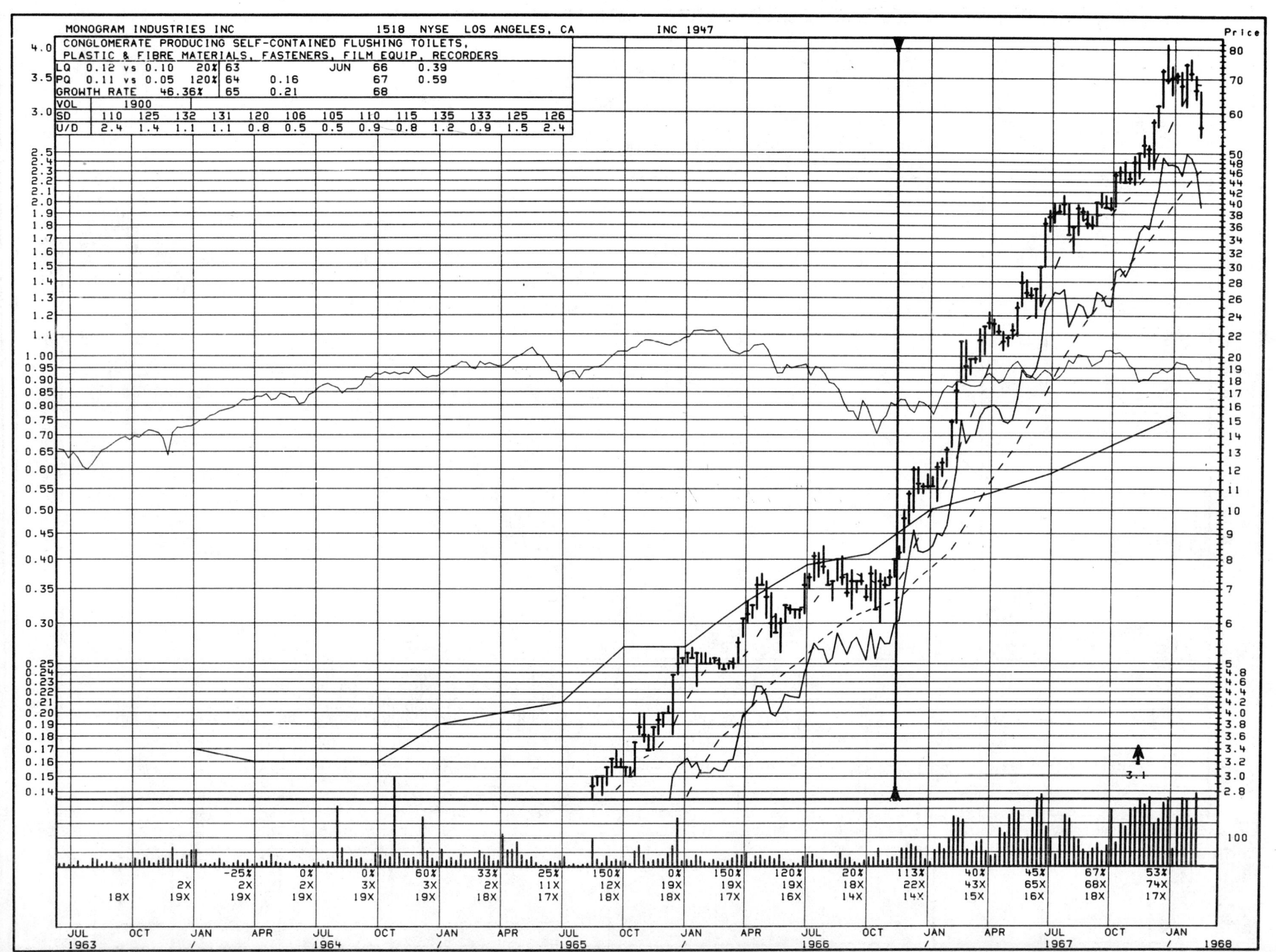

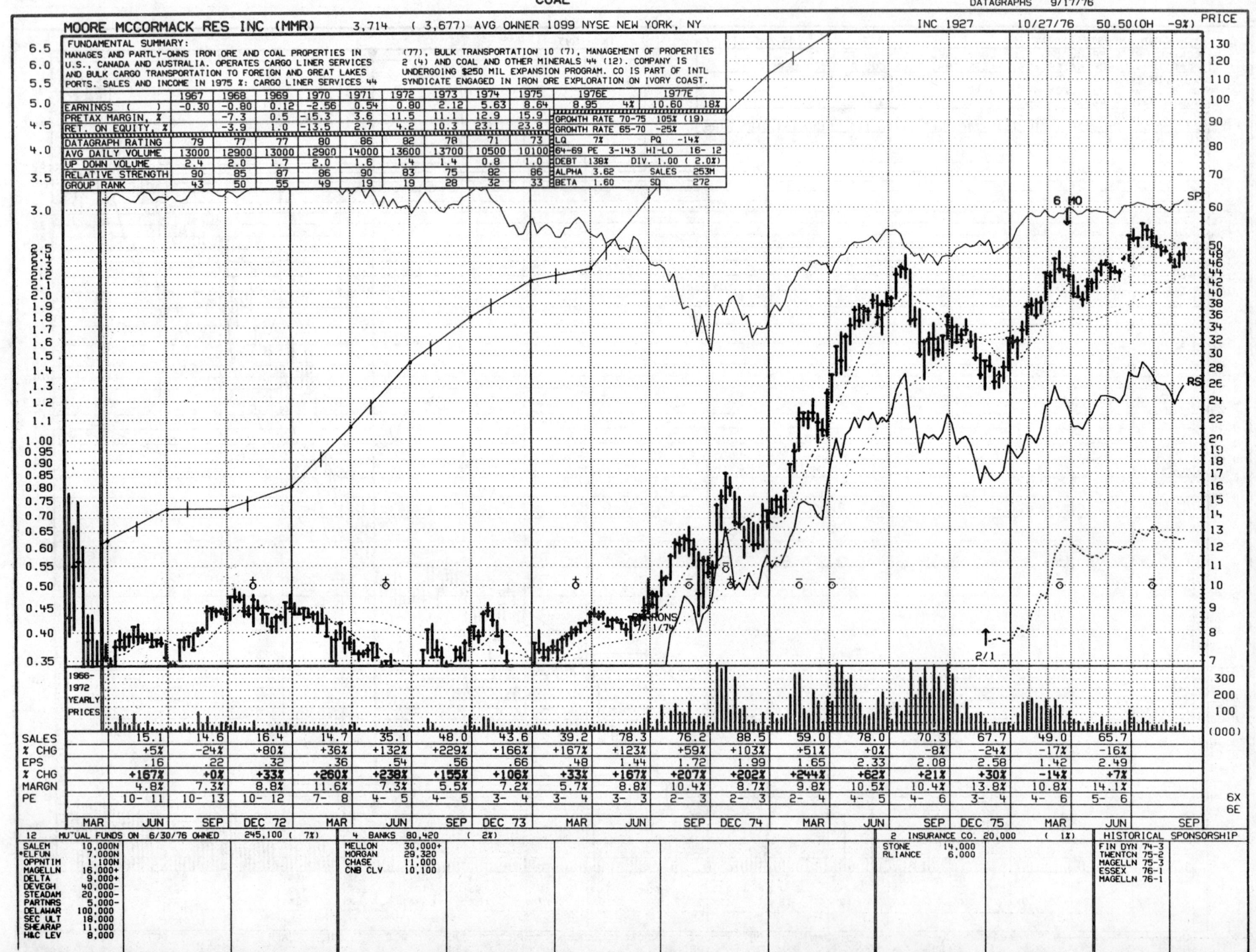

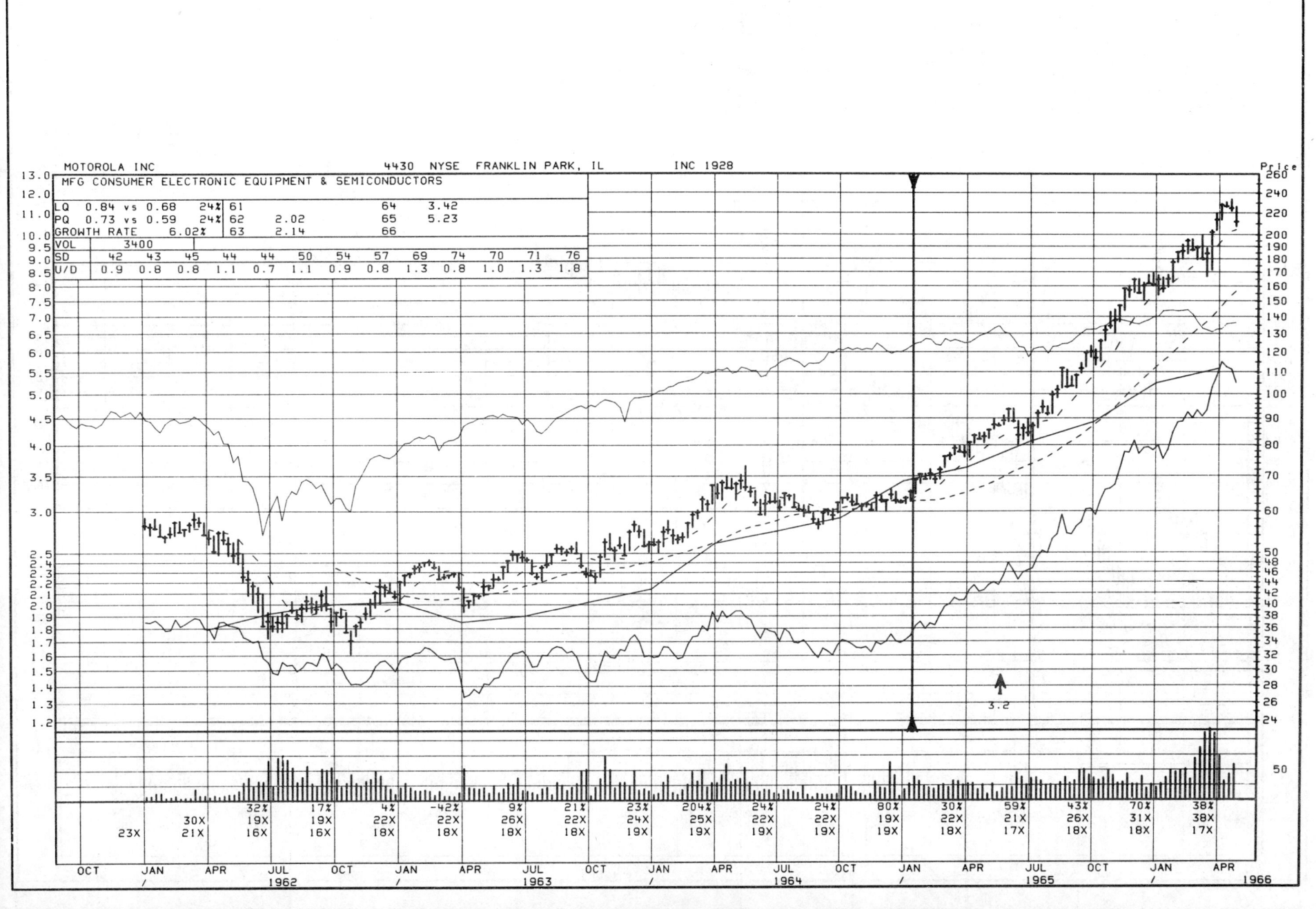

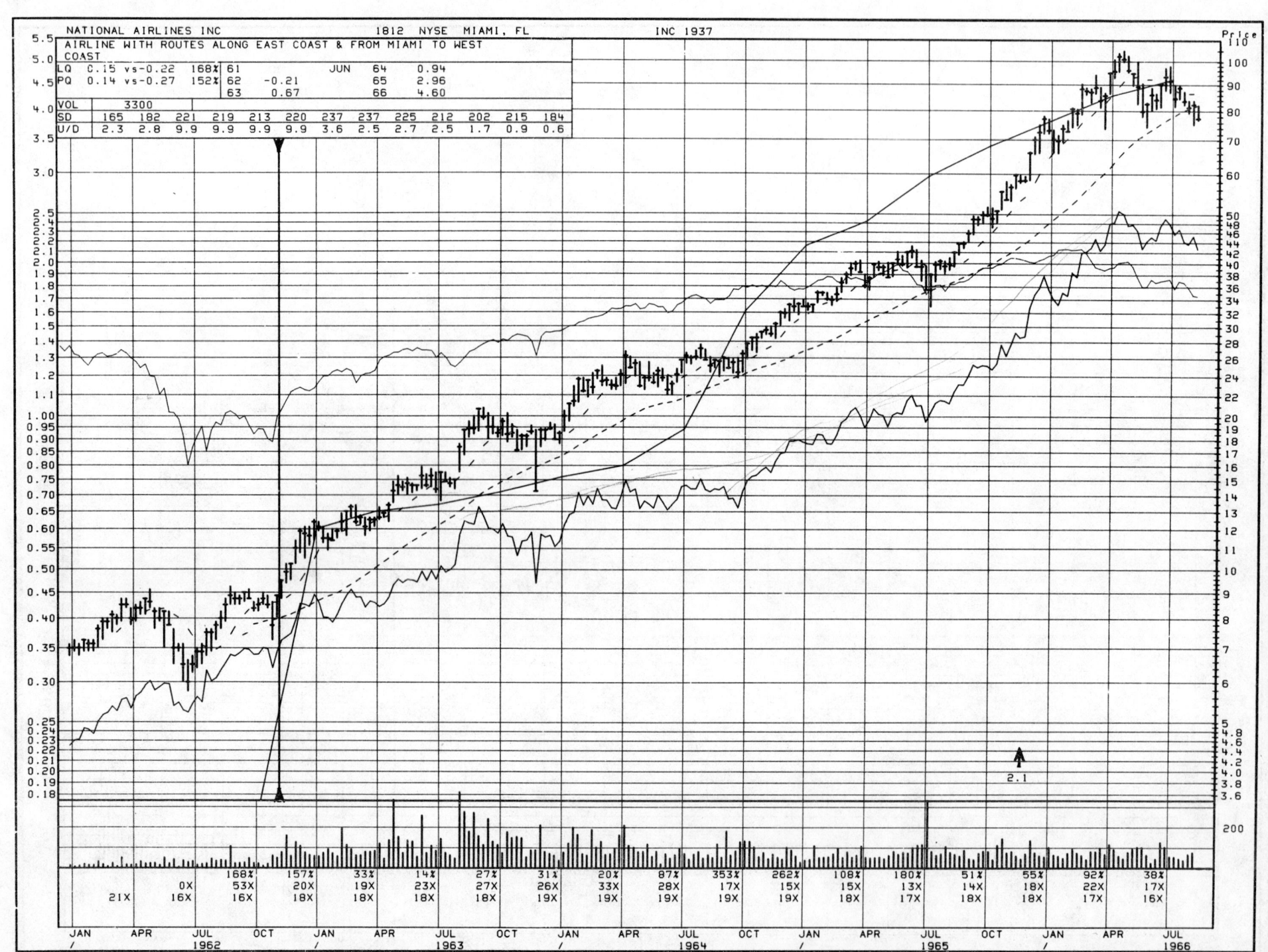

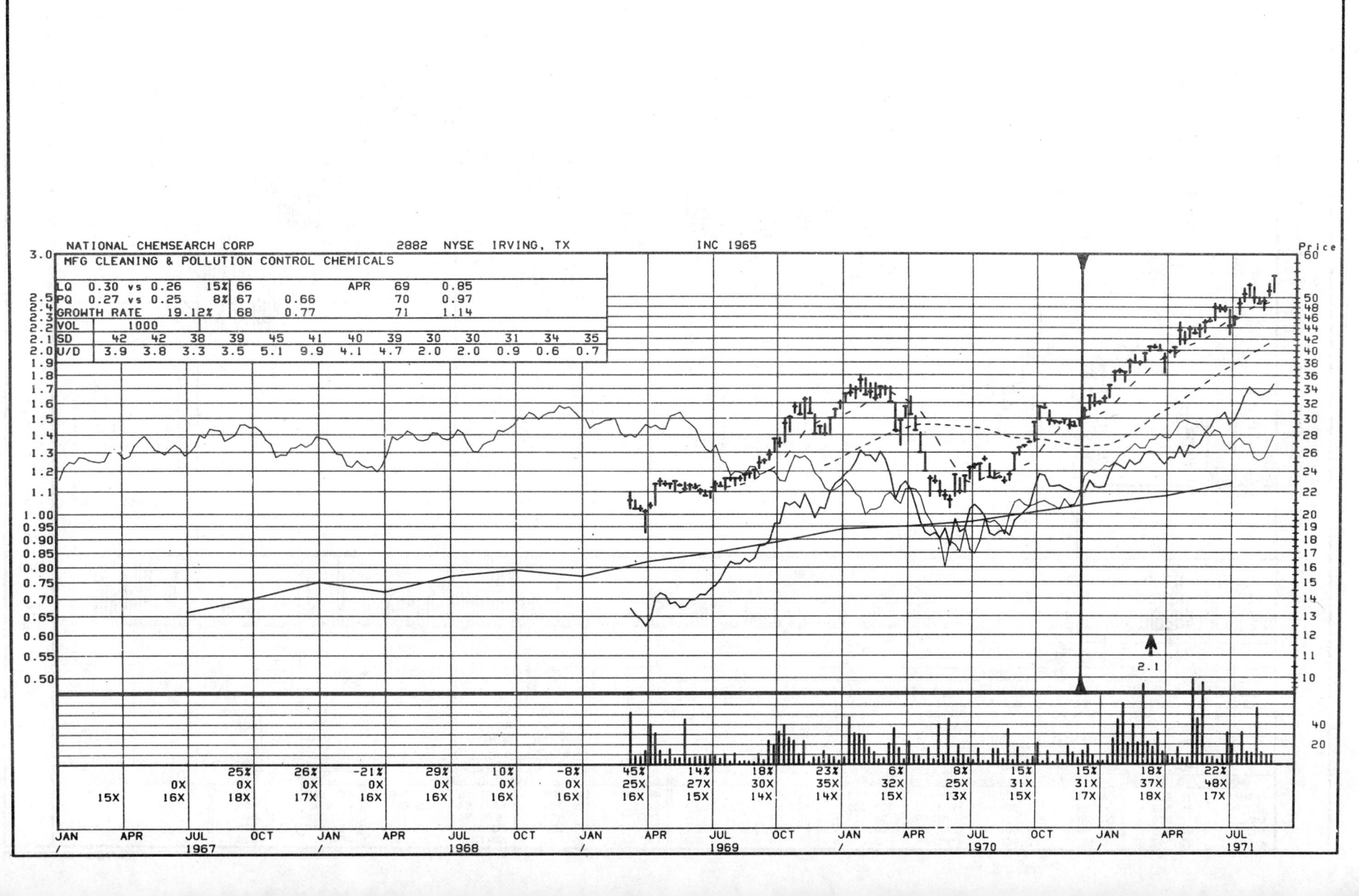

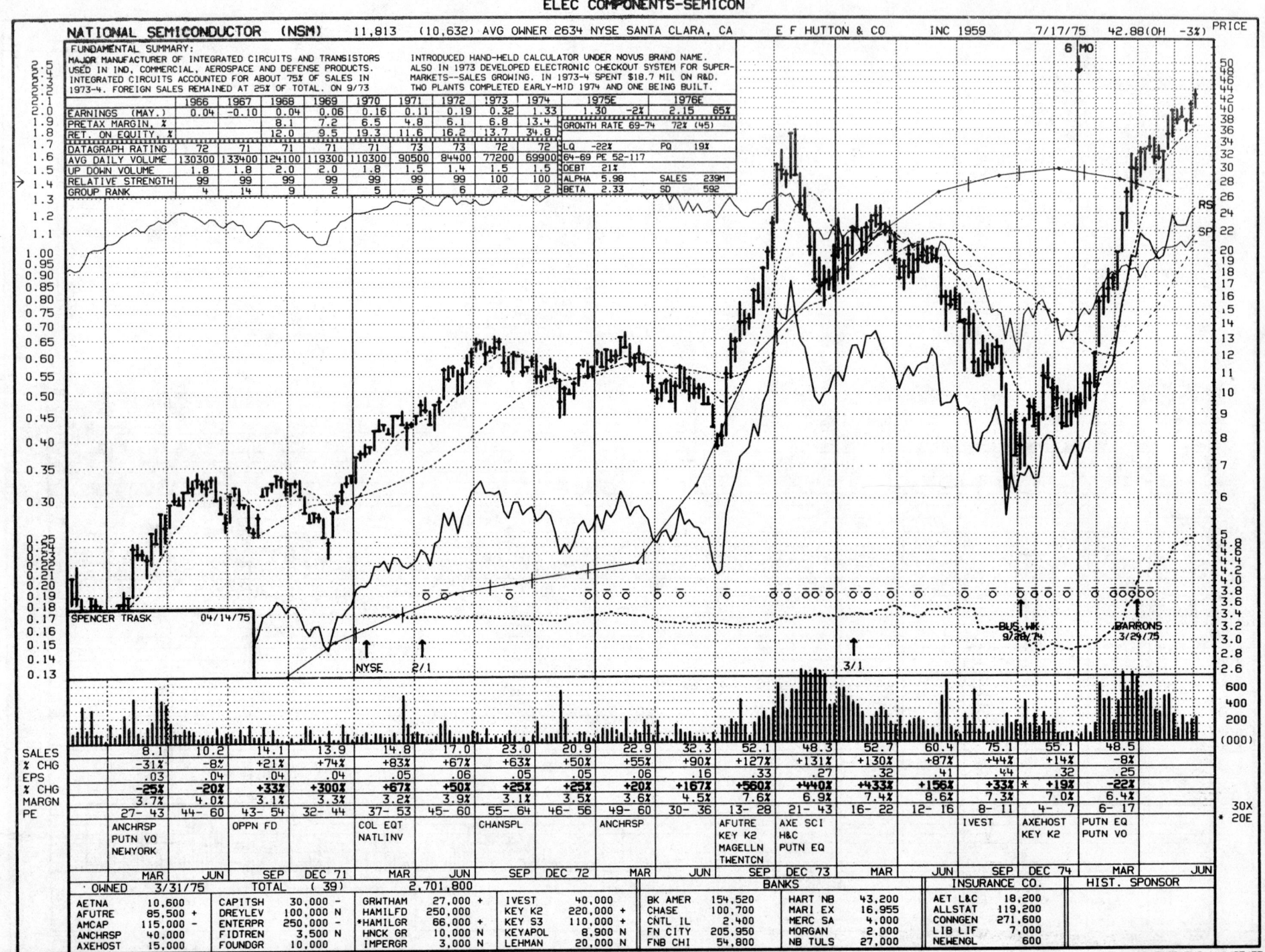

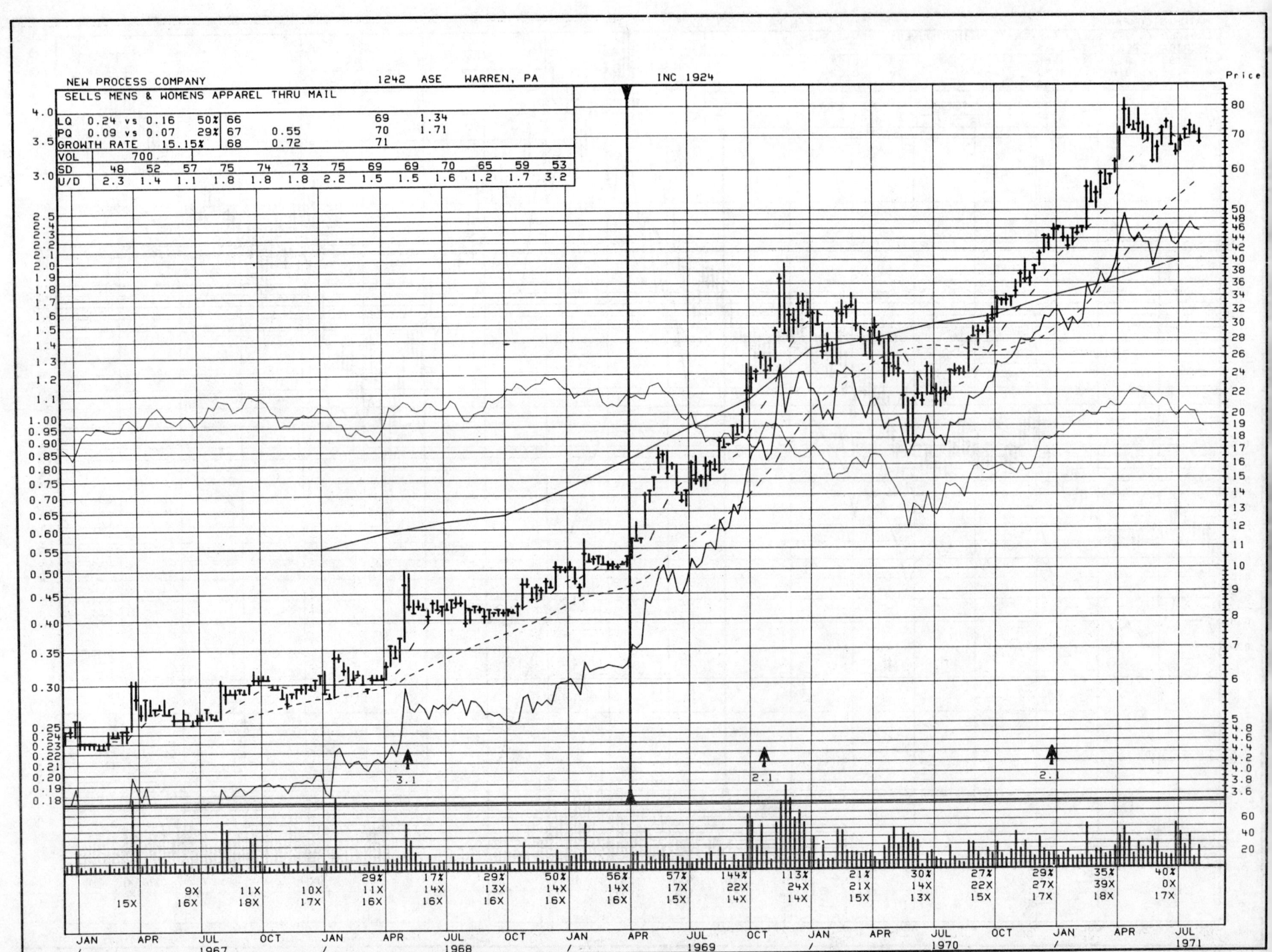

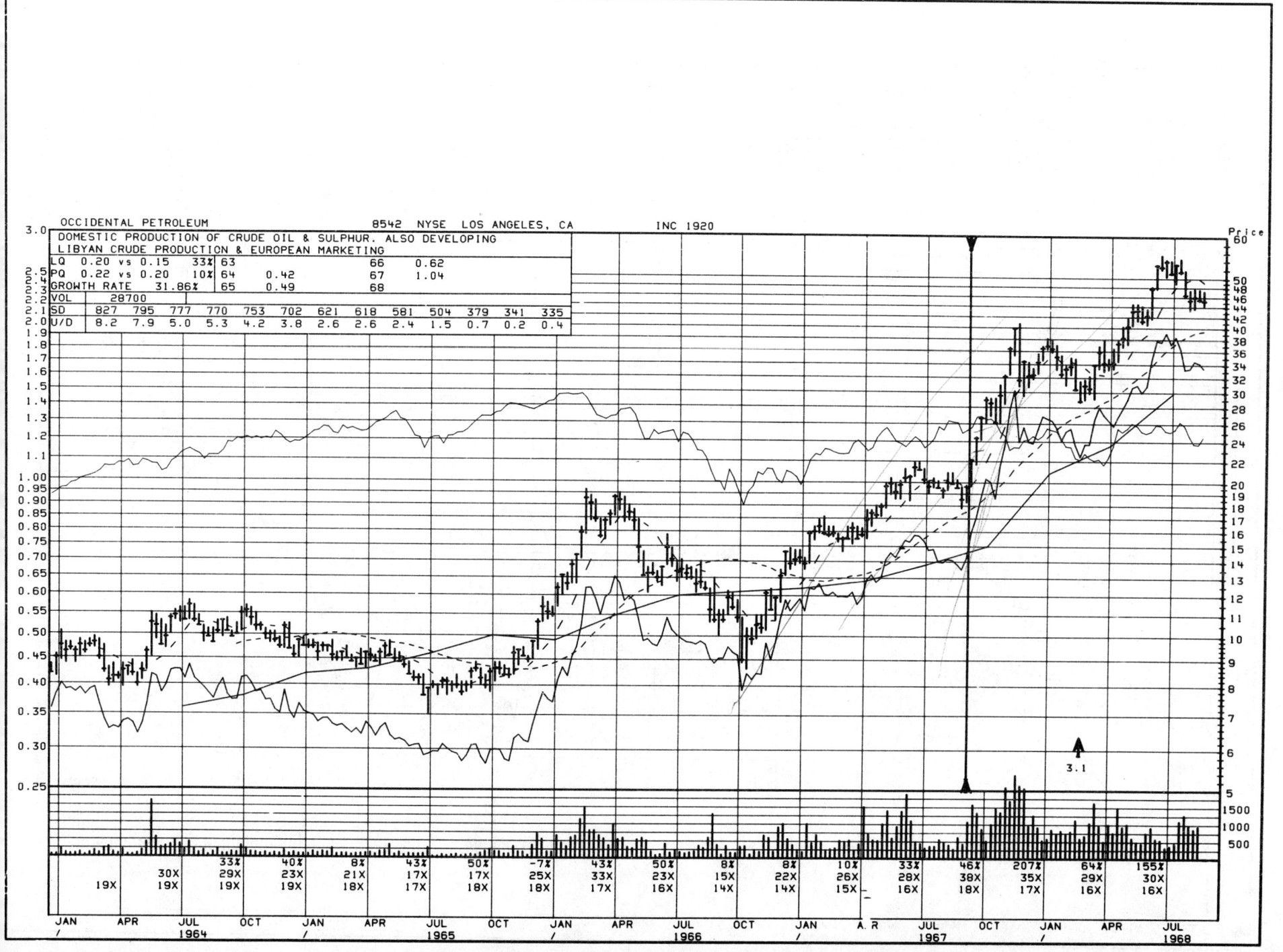

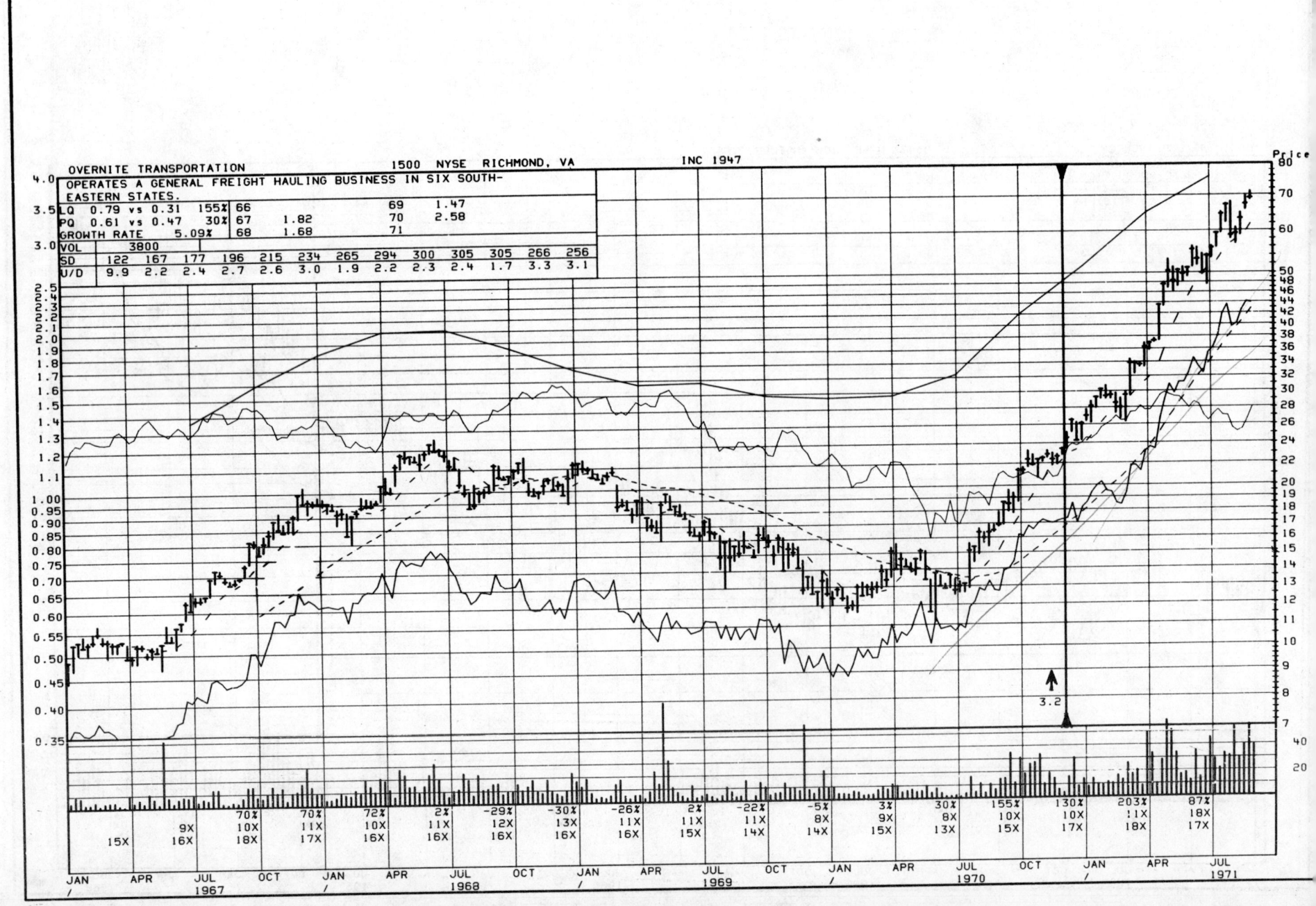

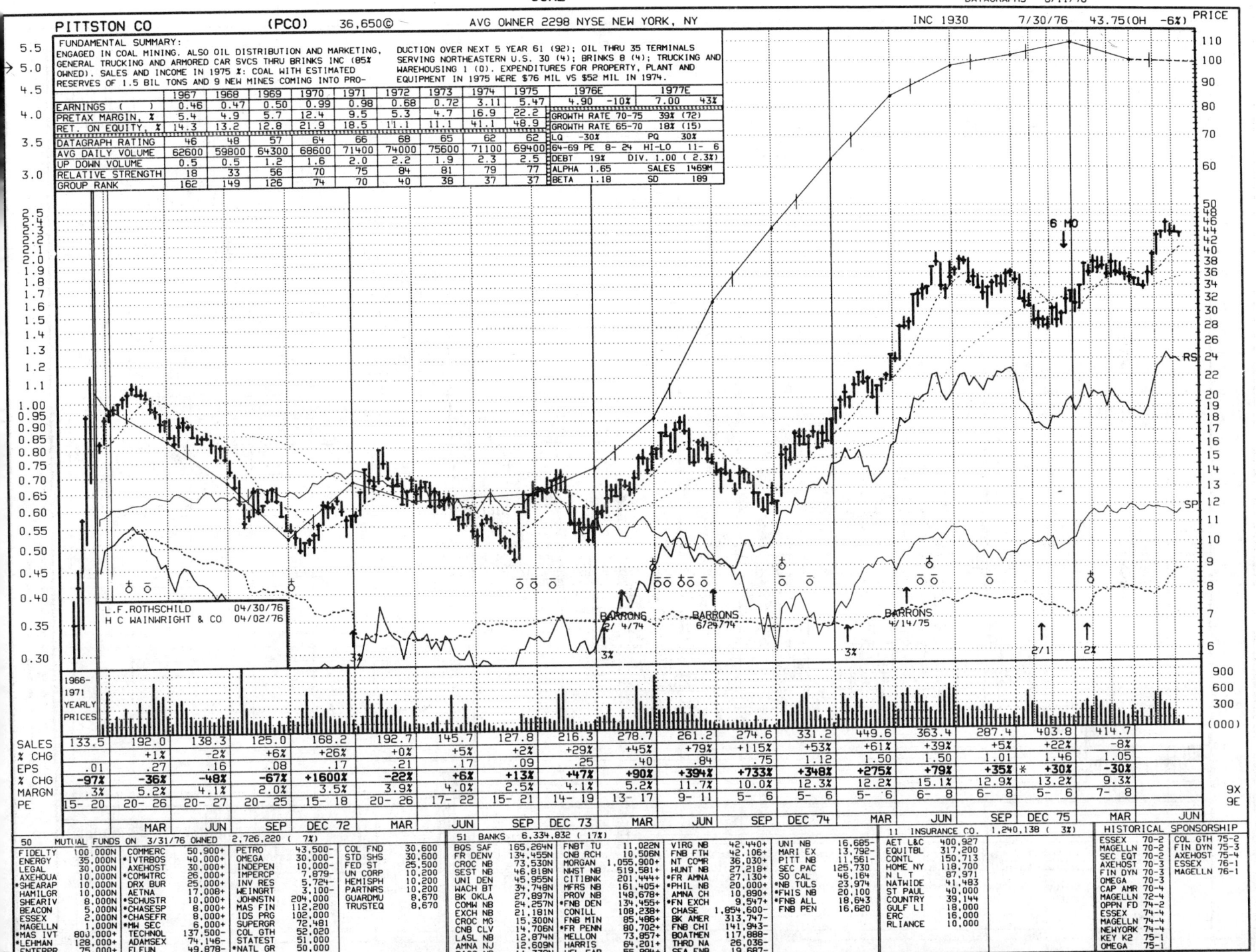

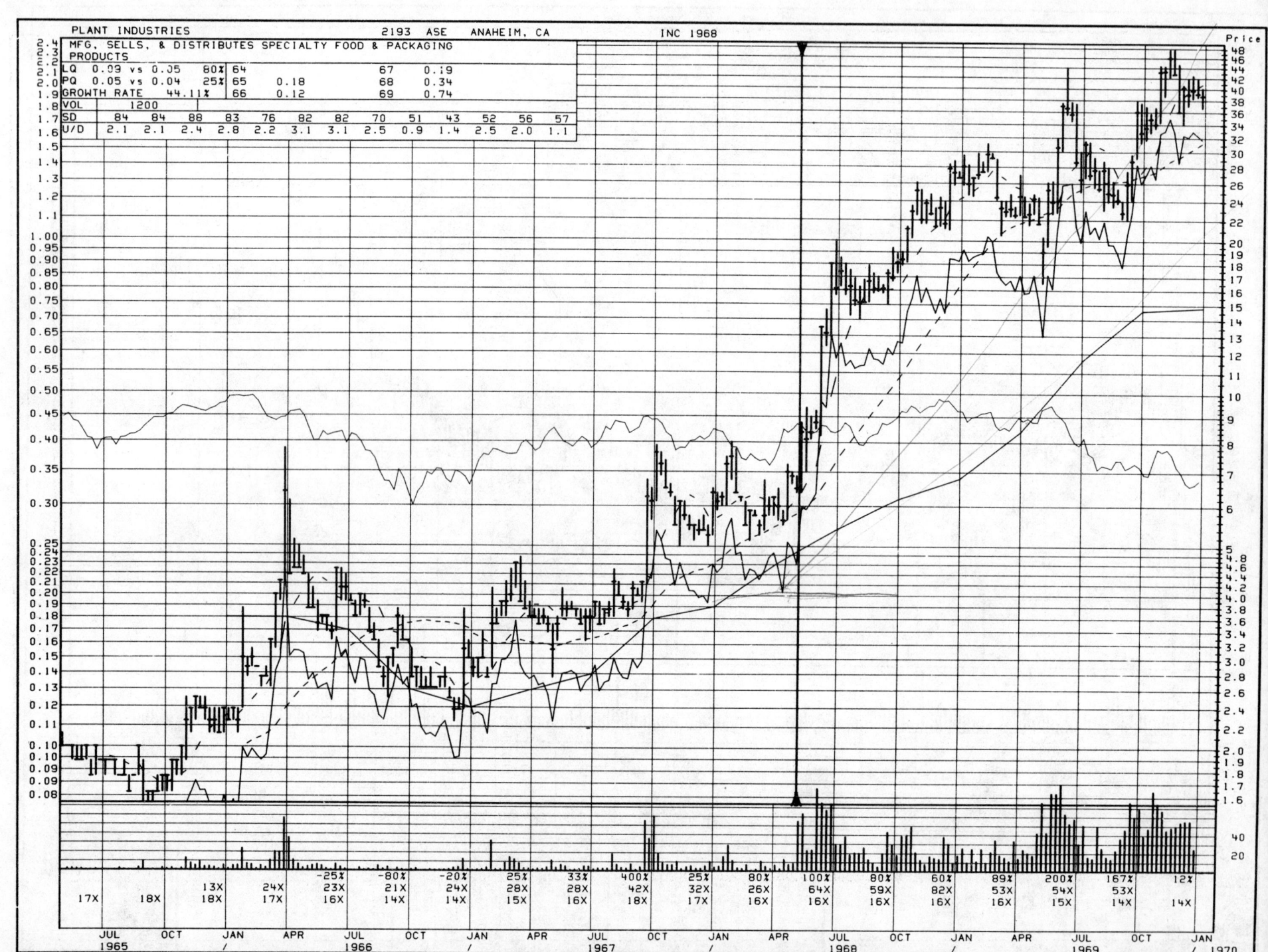

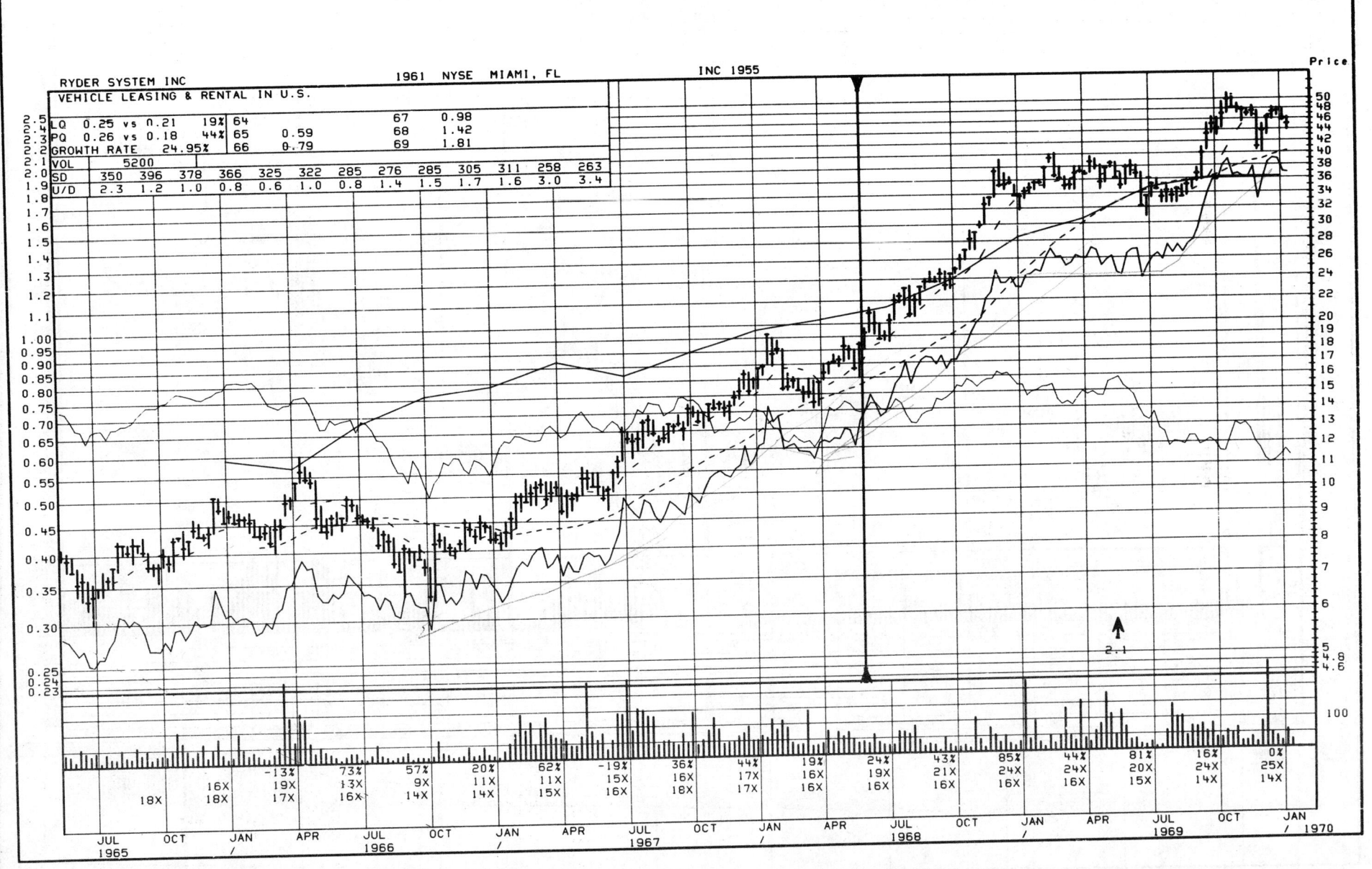

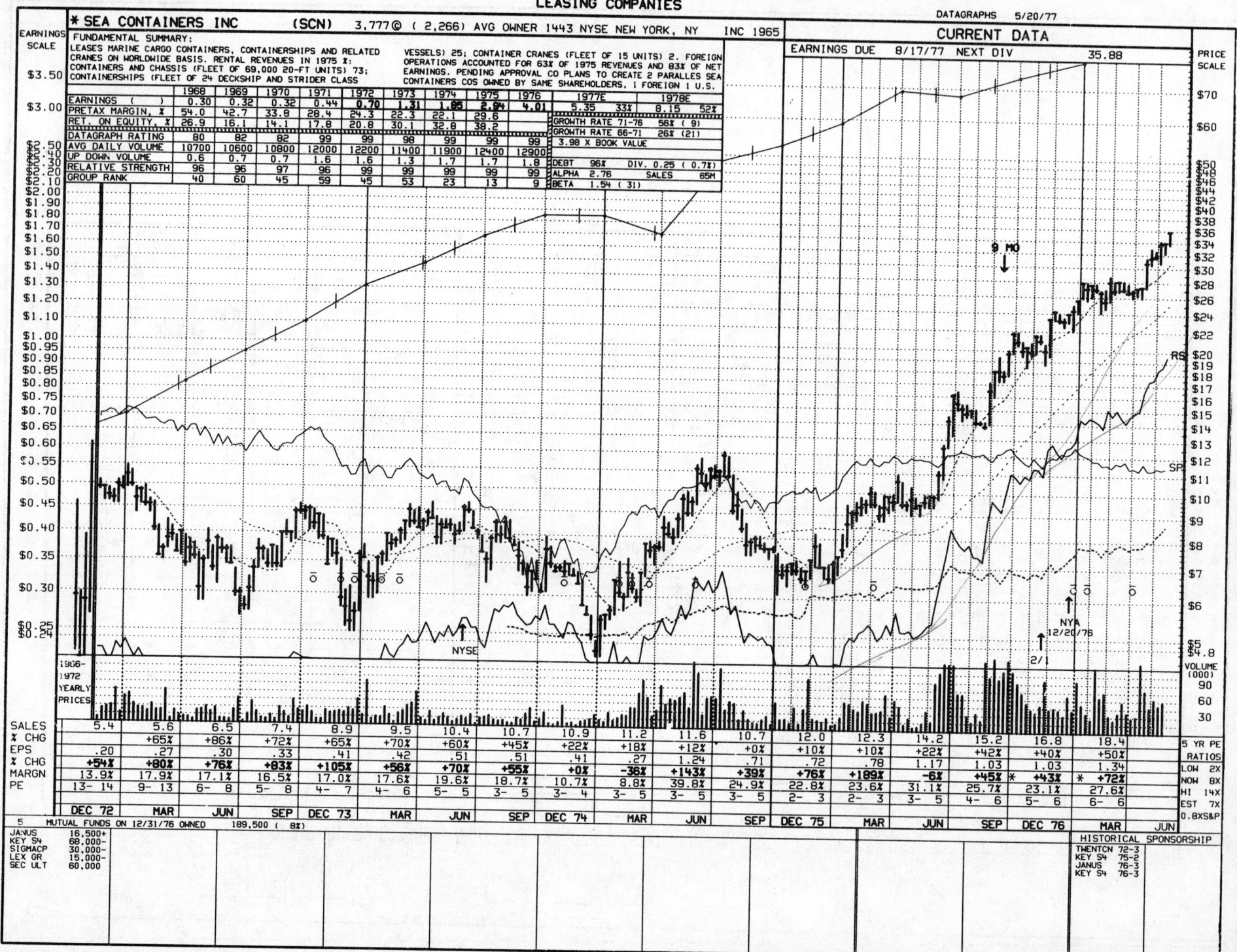

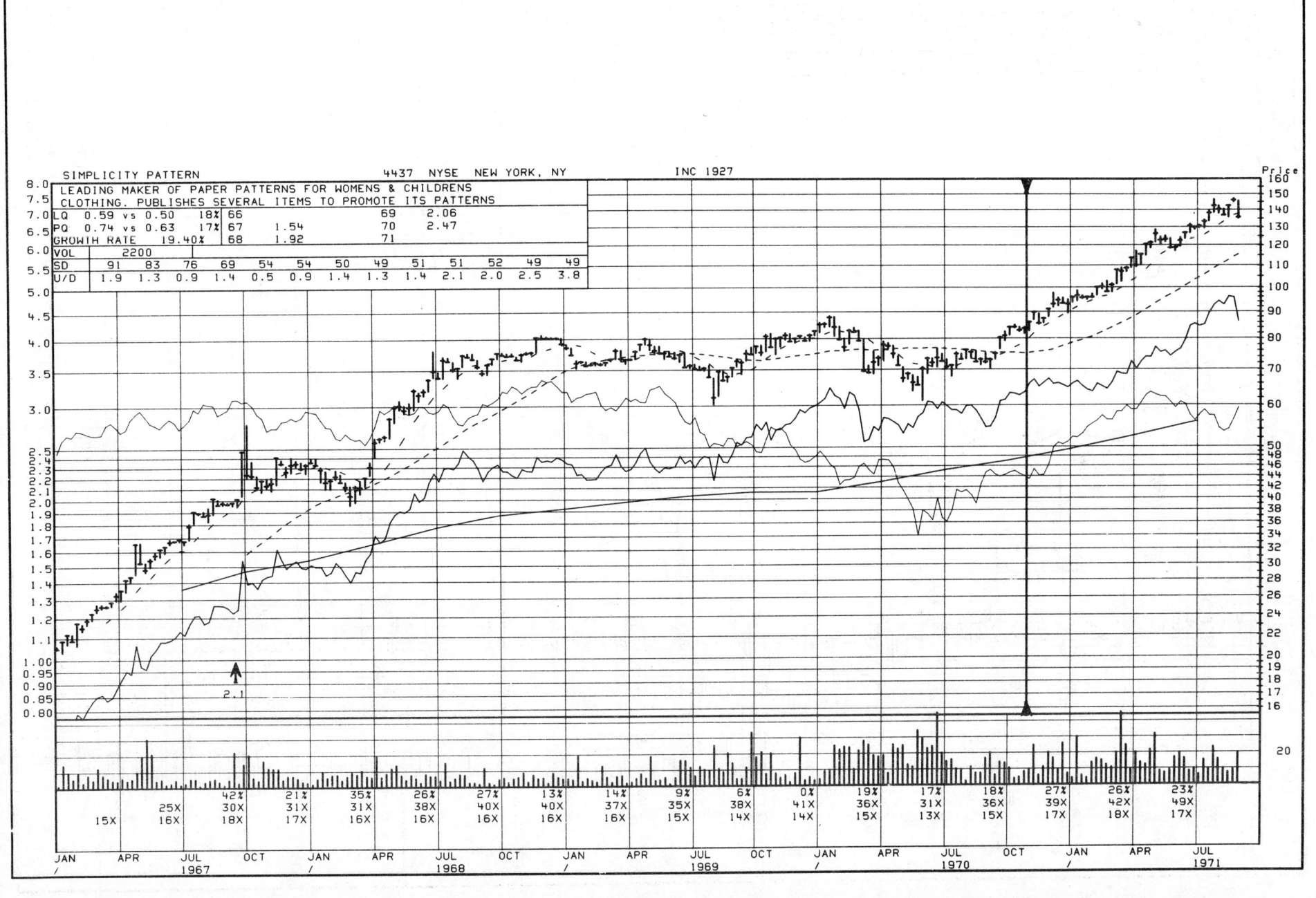

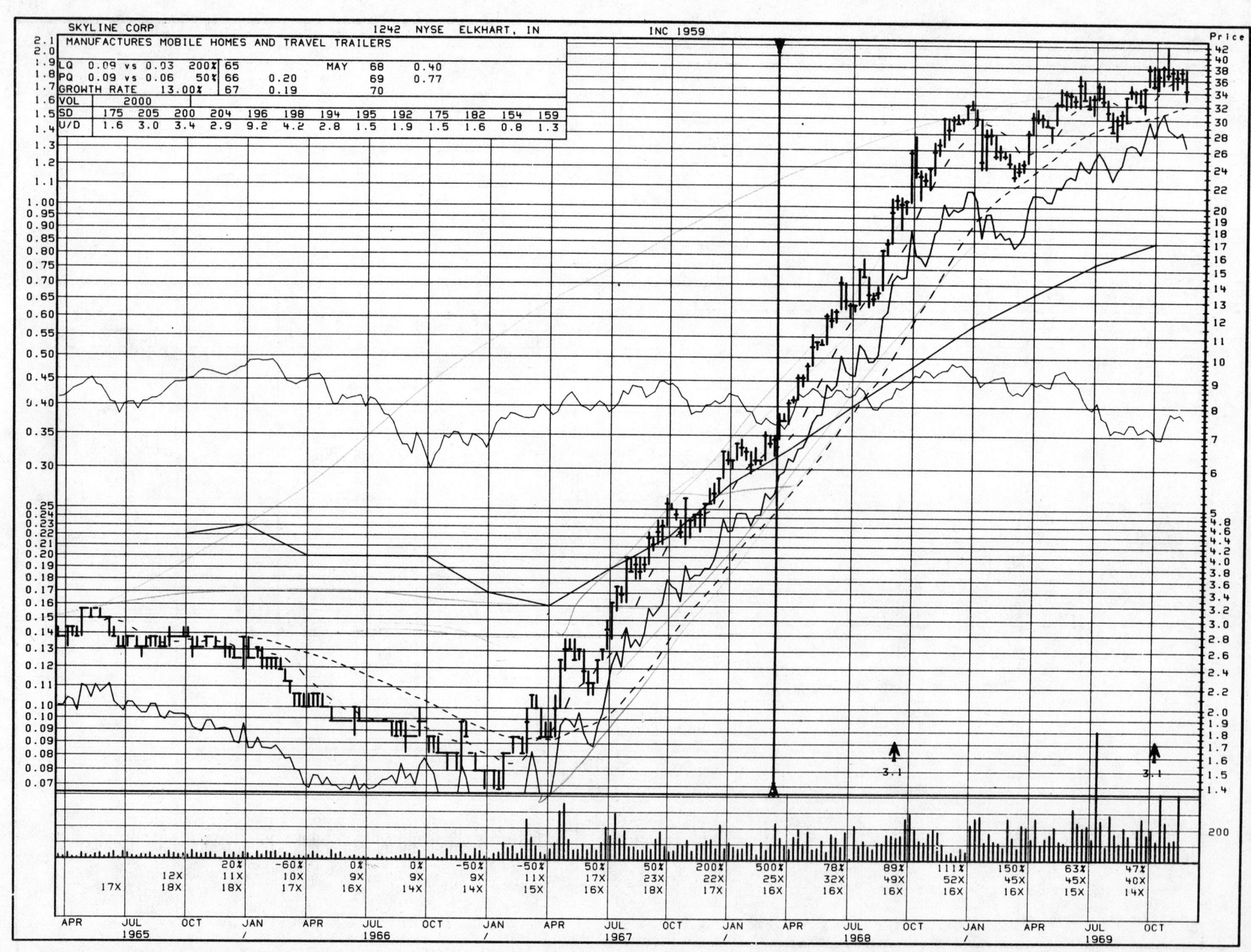

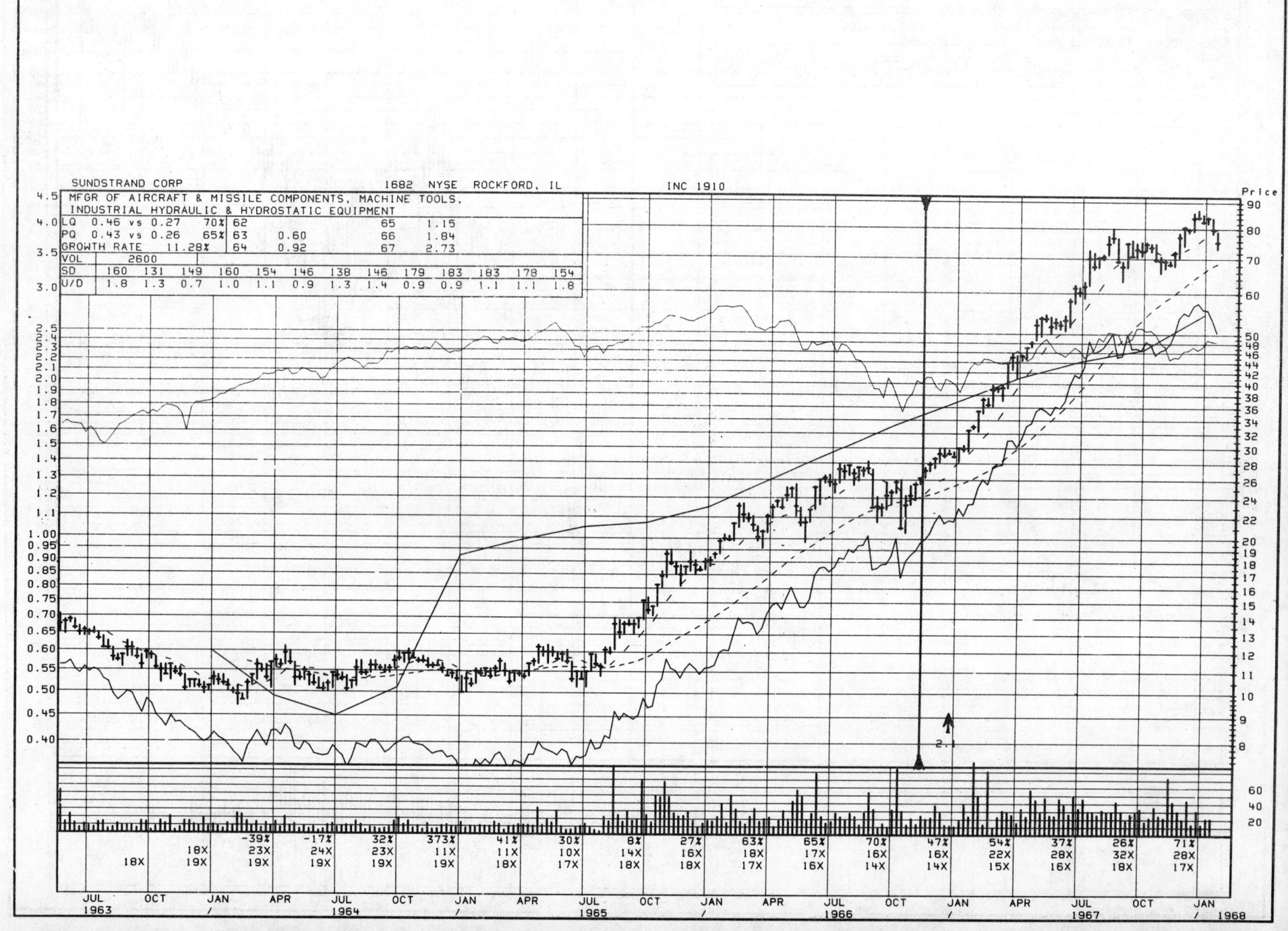

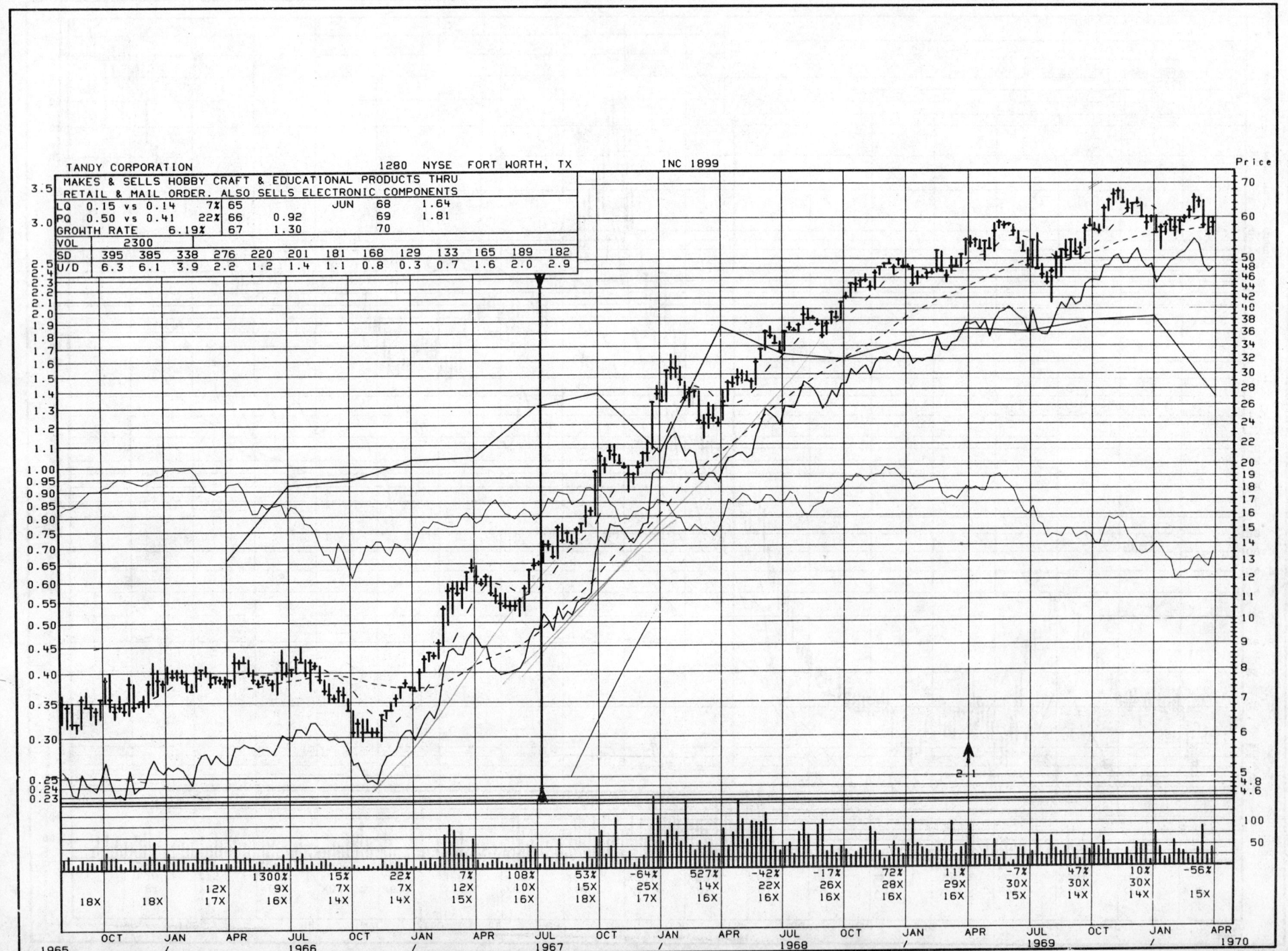

MEDICAL INSTRUMENTS

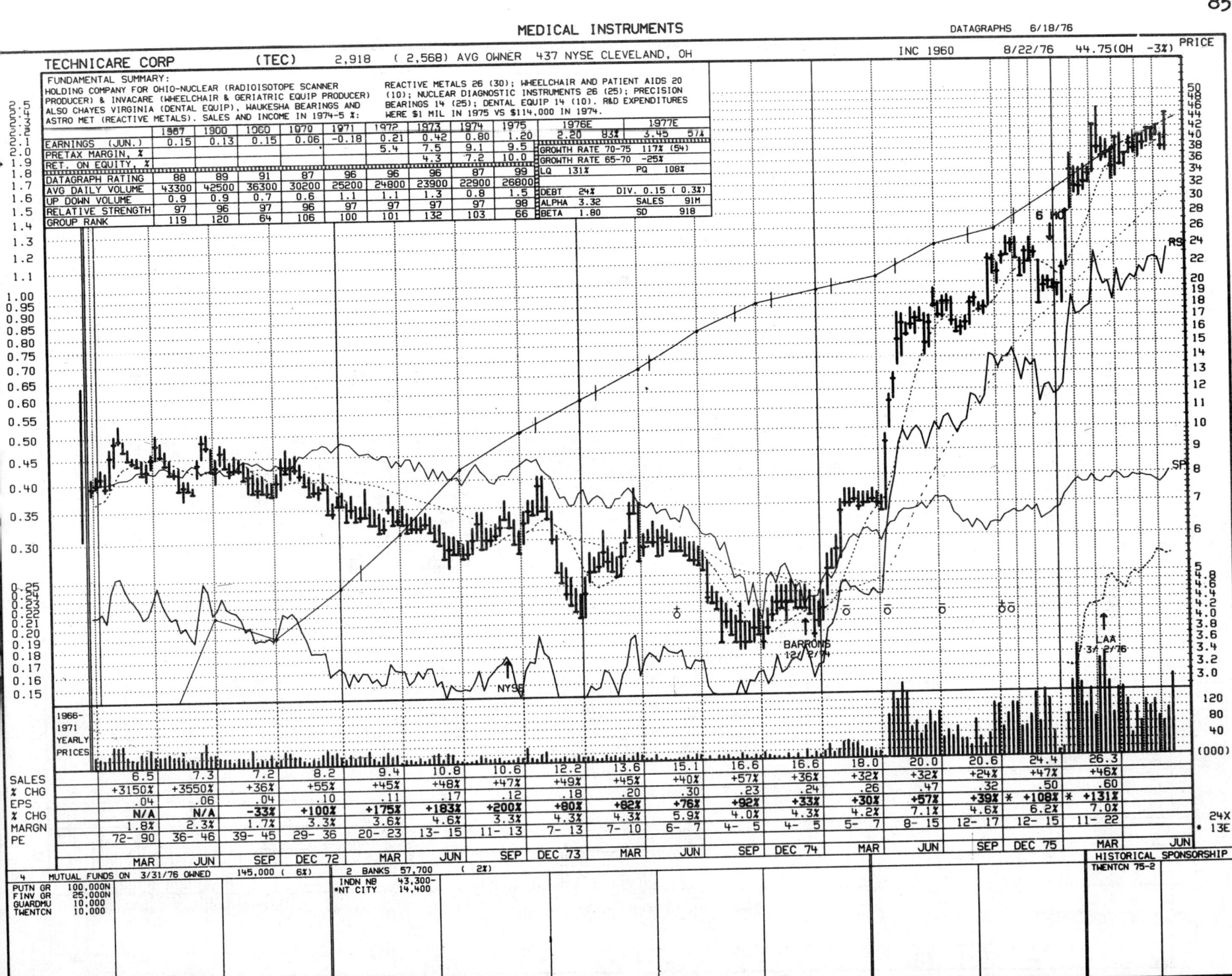

DATAGRAPHS 6/18/76

TECHNICARE CORP (TEC) 2,918 (2,568) AVG OWNER 437 NYSE CLEVELAND, OH
INC 1960   8/22/76   44.75(OH -3%)   PRICE

FUNDAMENTAL SUMMARY:
HOLDING COMPANY FOR OHIO-NUCLEAR (RADIOISOTOPE SCANNER PRODUCER) & INVACARE (WHEELCHAIR & GERIATRIC EQUIP PRODUCER) ALSO CHAYES VIRGINIA (DENTAL EQUIP), WAUKESHA BEARINGS AND ASTRO MET (REACTIVE METALS). SALES AND INCOME IN 1974-5 %: REACTIVE METALS 26 (30); WHEELCHAIR AND PATIENT AIDS 20 (10); NUCLEAR DIAGNOSTIC INSTRUMENTS 26 (25); PRECISION BEARINGS 14 (25); DENTAL EQUIP 14 (10). R&D EXPENDITURES WERE $1 MIL IN 1975 VS $114,000 IN 1974.

	1967	1968	1969	1970	1971	1972	1973	1974	1975	1976E	1977E
EARNINGS (JUN.)	0.15	0.13	0.15	0.06	-0.18	0.21	0.42	0.80	1.20	2.20 83%	3.45 57%
PRETAX MARGIN, %						5.4	7.5	9.1	9.5	GROWTH RATE 70-75 117% (54)	
RET. ON EQUITY, %							4.3	7.2	10.0	GROWTH RATE 65-70 -25%	
DATAGRAPH RATING	88	89	91	87	96	96	96	87	99	LQ 131% PQ 108%	
AVG DAILY VOLUME	43300	42500	36300	30200	25200	24800	23900	22900	26800	DEBT 24% DIV. 0.15 (0.3%)	
UP DOWN VOLUME	0.9	0.9	0.7	0.6	1.1	1.1	1.3	0.8	1.5	ALPHA 3.32 SALES 91M	
RELATIVE STRENGTH	97	96	97	96	97	97	97	98	97	BETA 1.80 SD 918	
GROUP RANK	119	120	64	106	100	101	132	103	66		

SALES	6.5	7.3	7.2	8.2	9.4	10.8	10.6	12.2	13.6	15.1	16.6	16.6	18.0	20.0	20.6	24.4	26.3
% CHG	+3150%	+3550%	+36%	+55%	+45%	+48%	+47%	+49%	+45%	+40%	+57%	+36%	+32%	+32%	+24%	+47%	+46%
EPS	.04	.06		.10	.11	.17	.12	.18	.20	.30	.23	.24	.26	.47	.32	.50	.60
% CHG	N/A	N/A	-33%	+100%	+175%	+183%	+200%	+80%	+82%	+76%	+92%	+33%	+30%	+57%	+39%	+108%	+131%
MARGN	1.8%	2.3%	1.7%	3.3%	3.6%	4.6%	3.3%	4.3%	4.3%	5.9%	4.0%	4.3%	4.2%	7.1%	4.6%	6.2%	7.0%
PE	72-90	36-46	39-45	29-36	20-23	13-15	11-13	7-13	7-10	6-7	4-5	4-5	5-7	8-15	12-17	12-15	11-22

24X *13E

| | MAR | JUN | SEP | DEC 72 | MAR | JUN | SEP | DEC 73 | MAR | JUN | SEP | DEC 74 | MAR | JUN | SEP | DEC 75 | MAR | JUN |

HISTORICAL SPONSORSHIP: TWENTCN 75-2

4 MUTUAL FUNDS ON 3/31/76 OWNED 145,000 (6%)   2 BANKS 57,700 (2%)
PUTN GR 100,000N   INDN NB 43,300
FINV GR 25,000N   *NT CITY 14,400
GUARDMU 10,000
TWENTCN 10,000

85

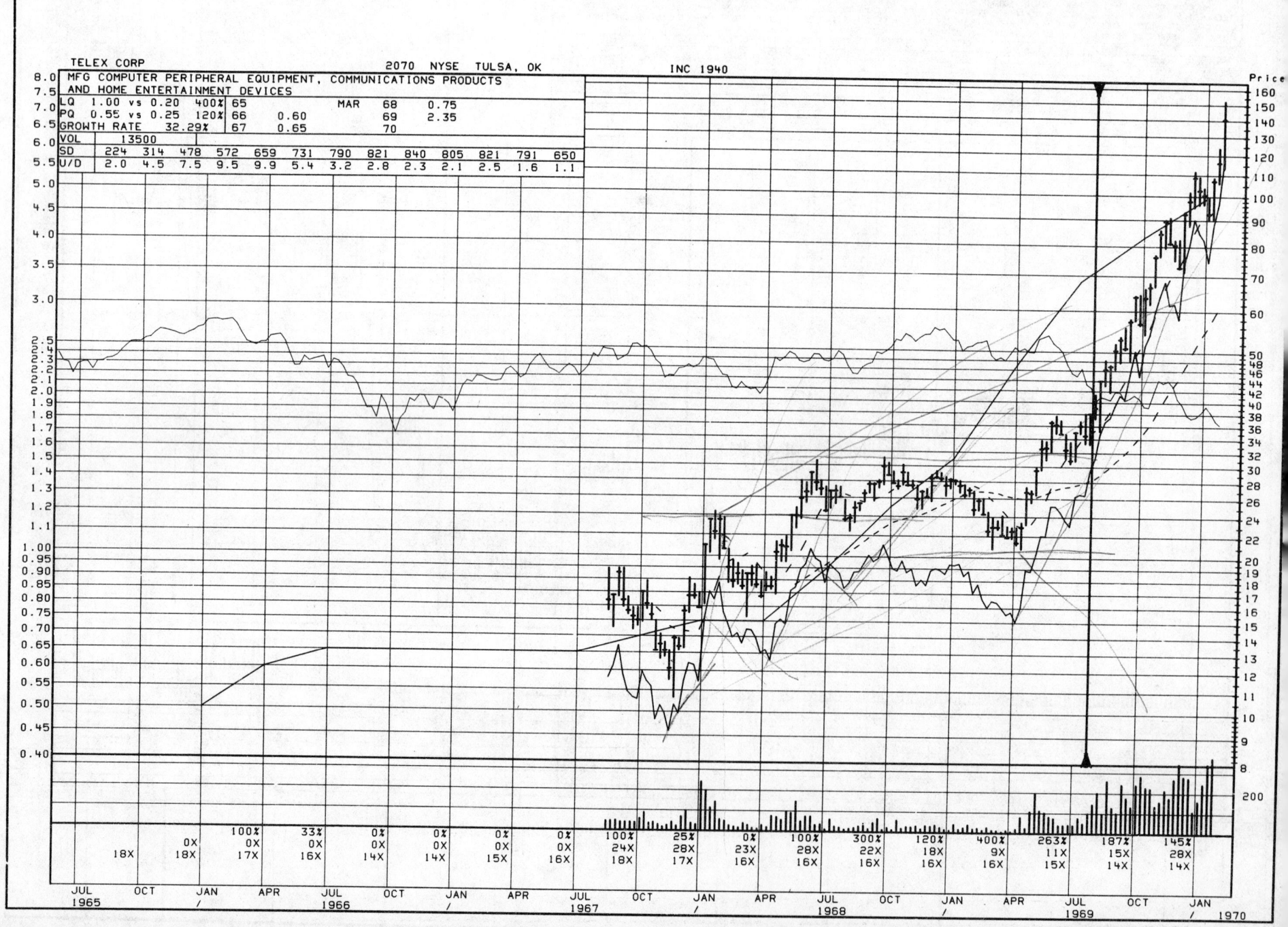

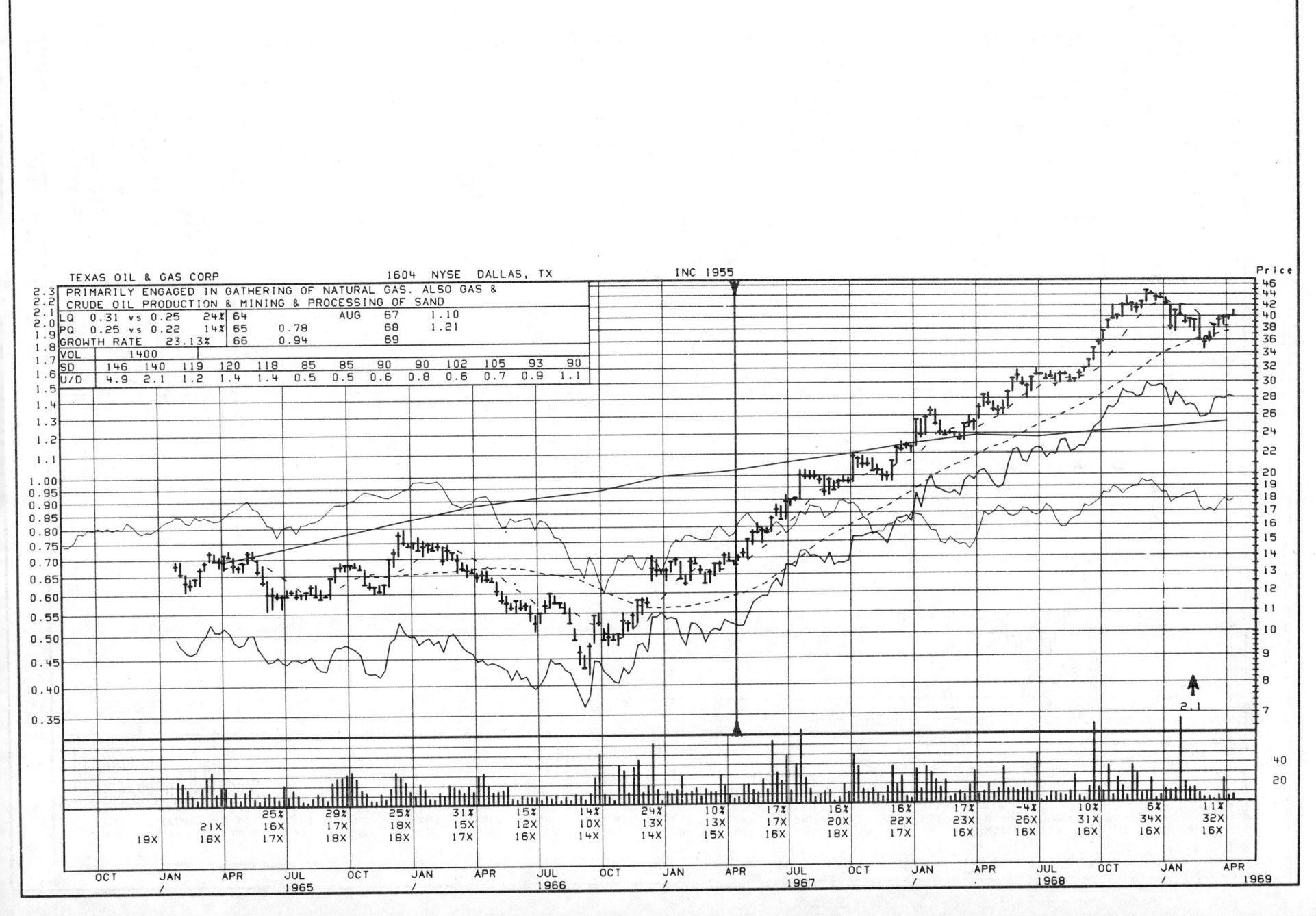

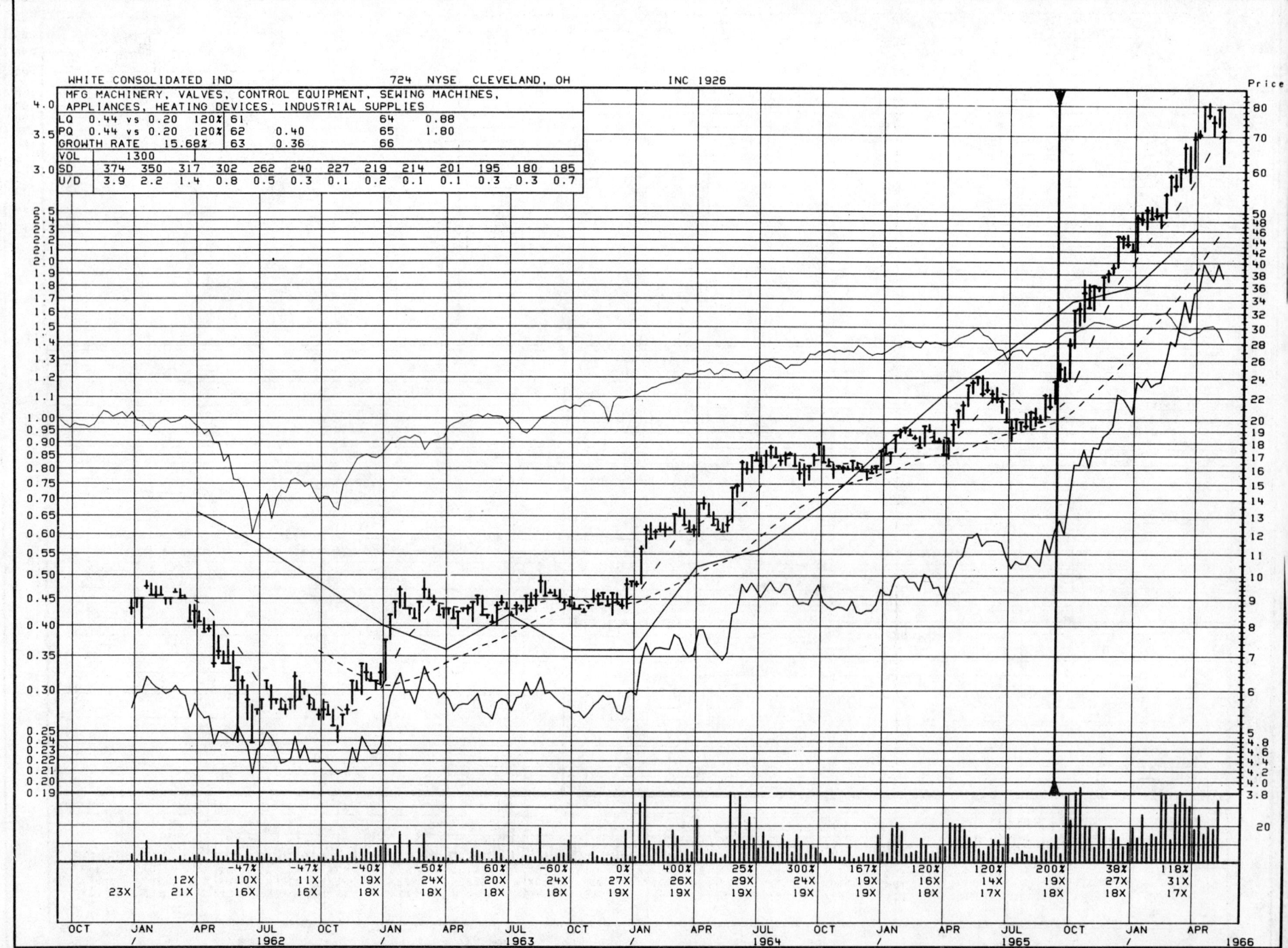

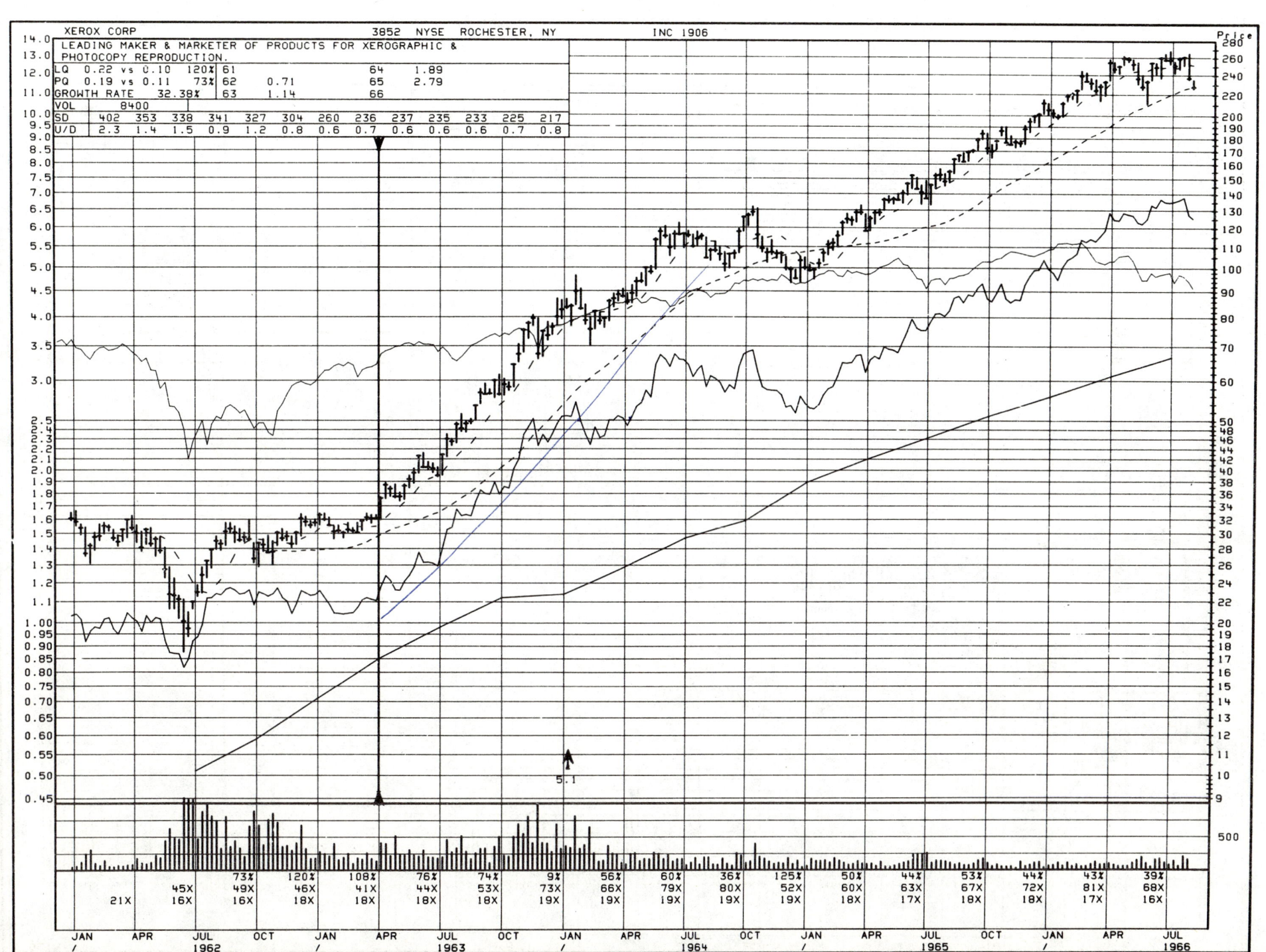

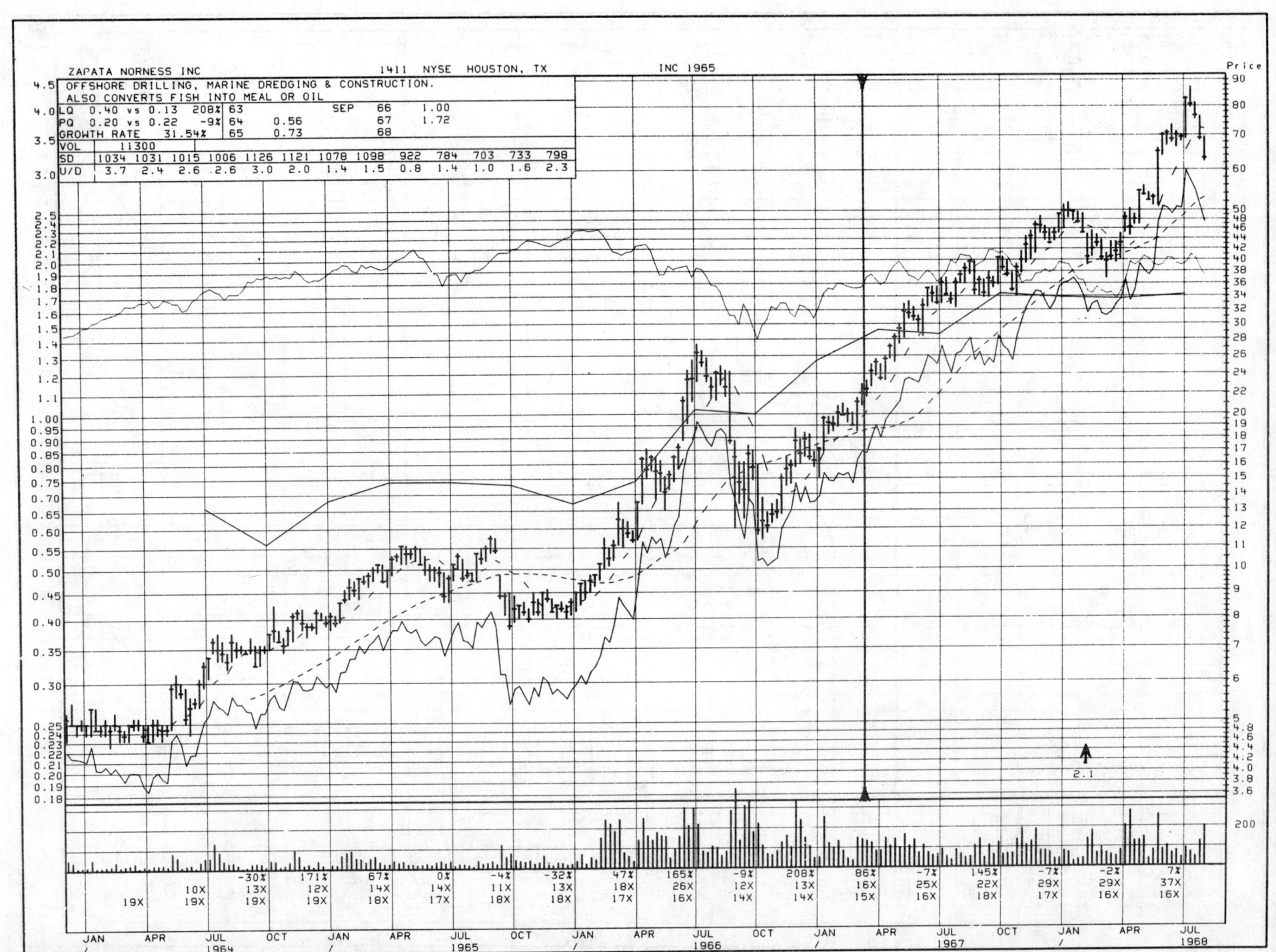

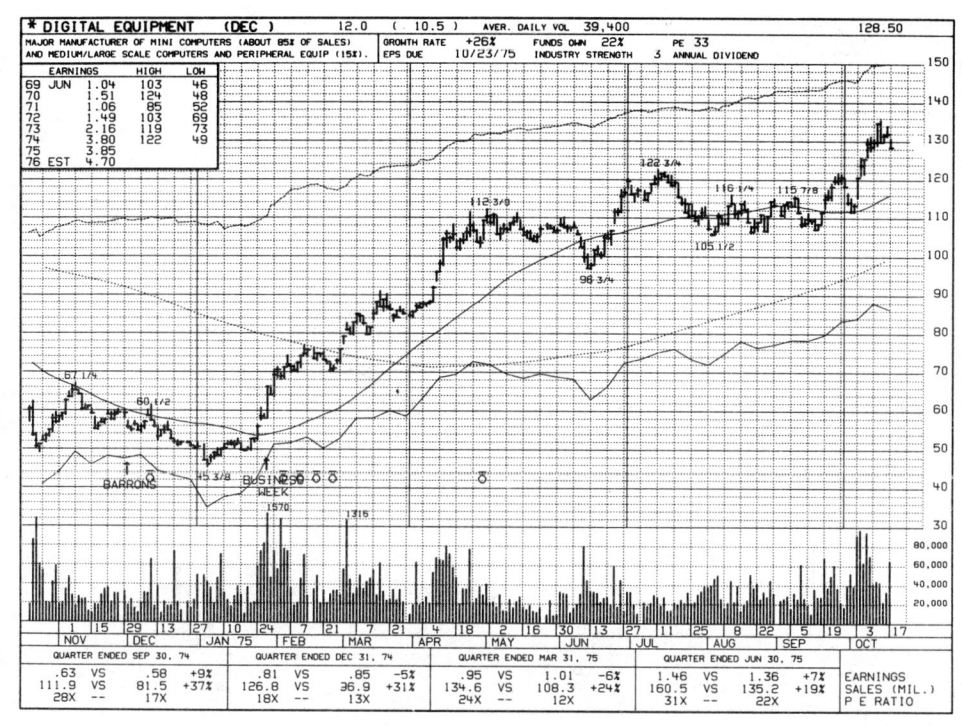
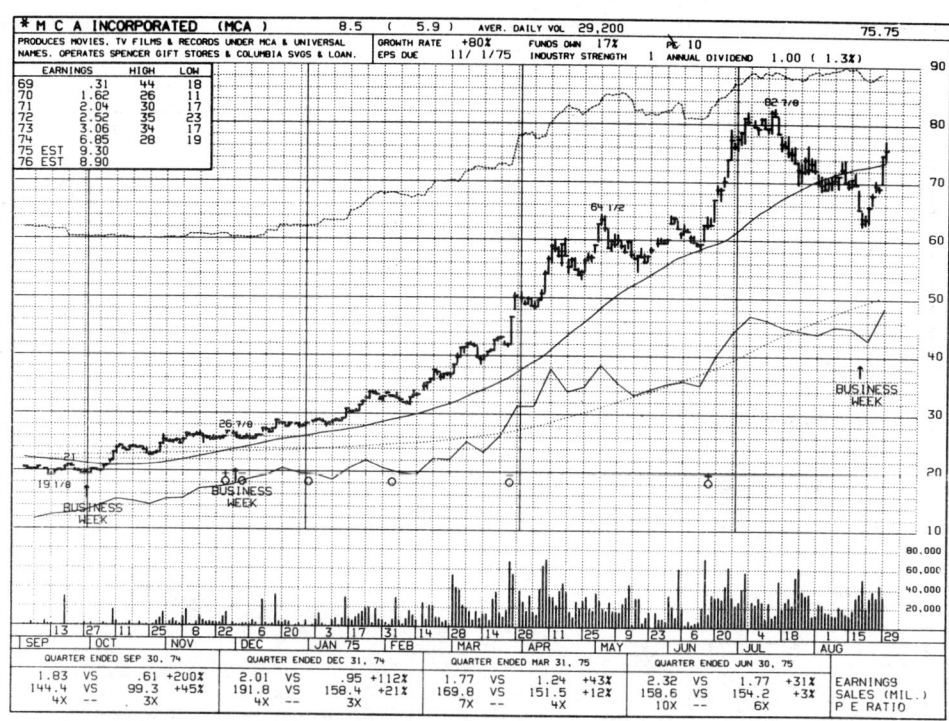
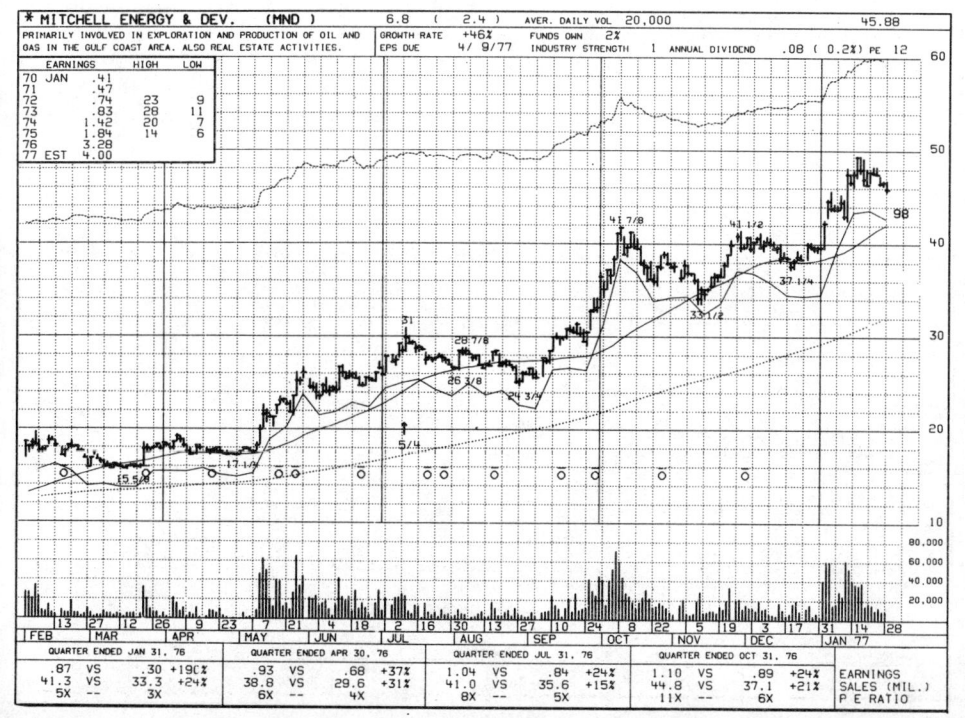
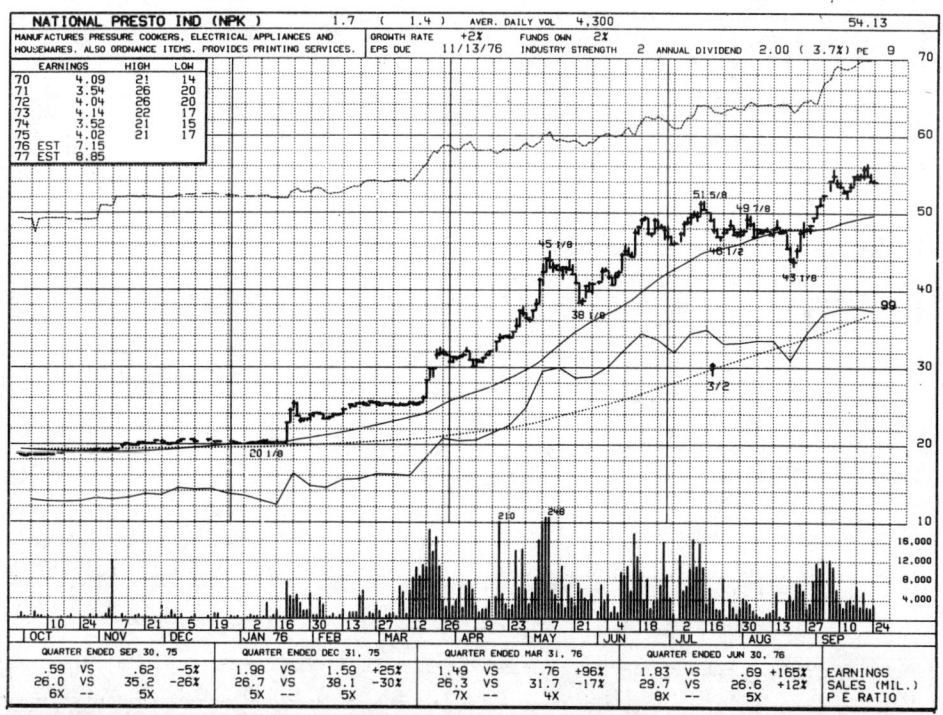

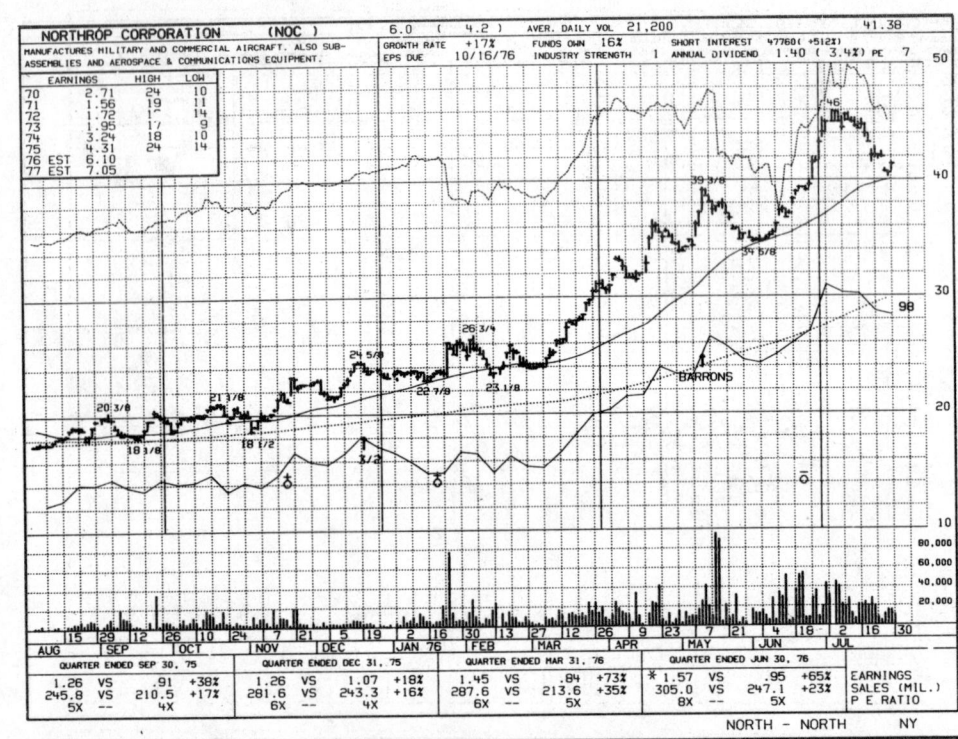
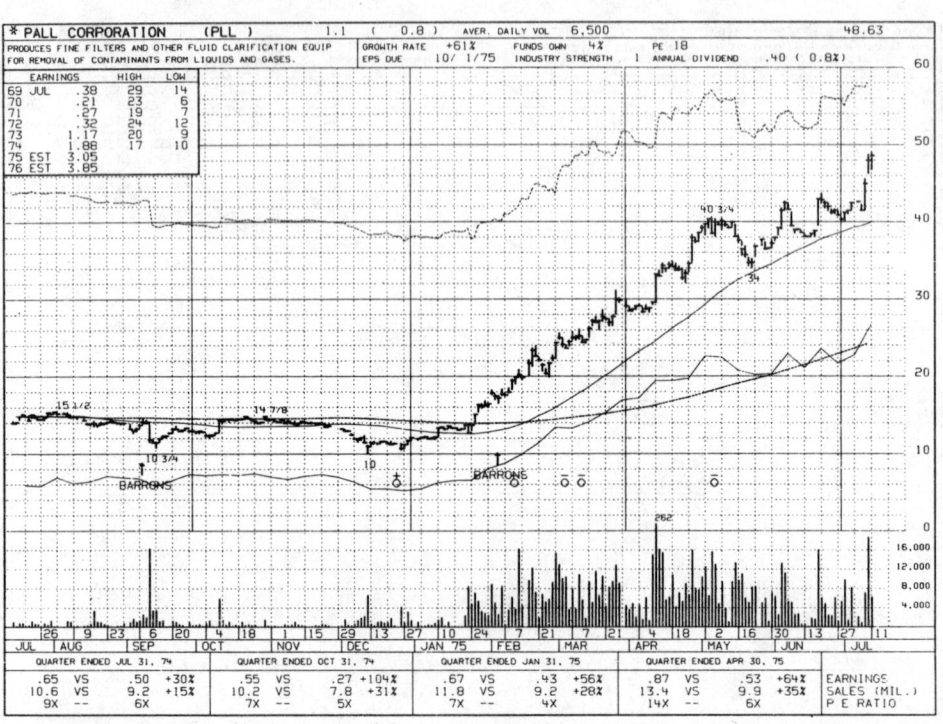
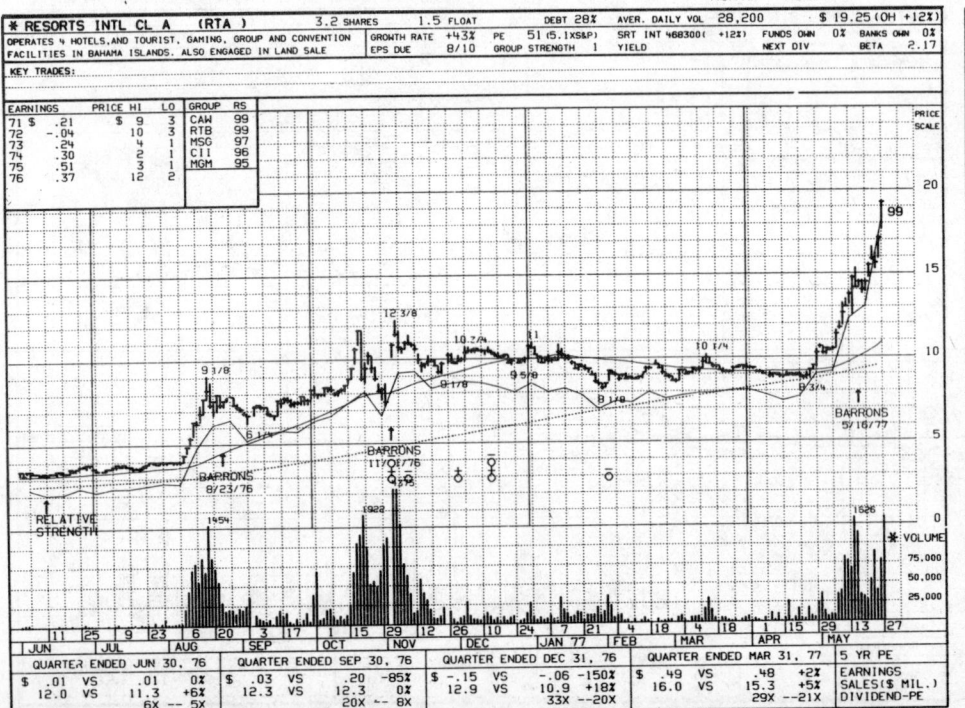
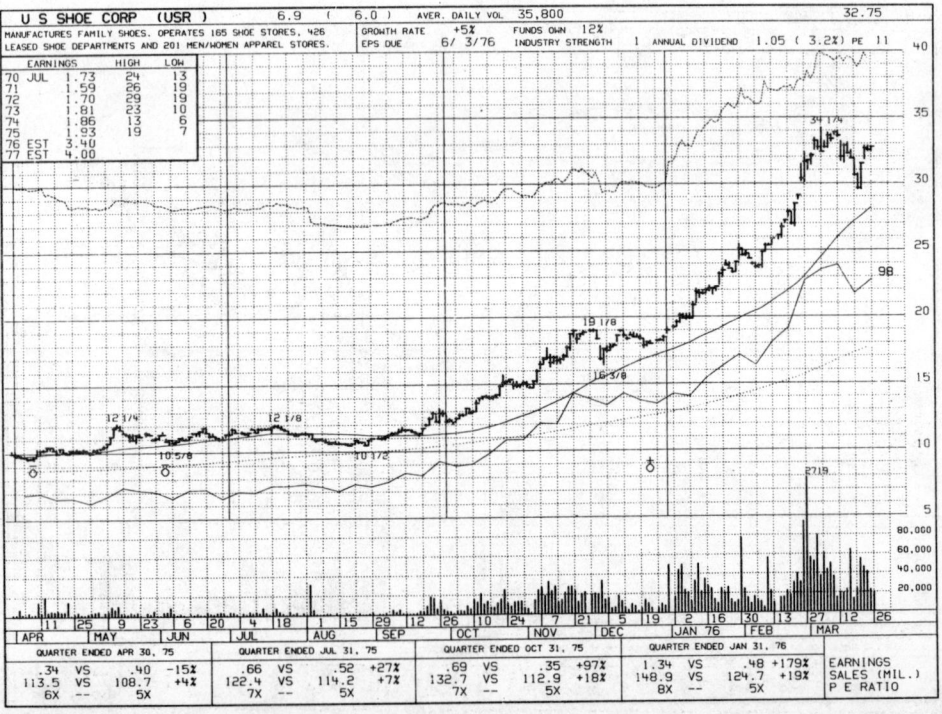

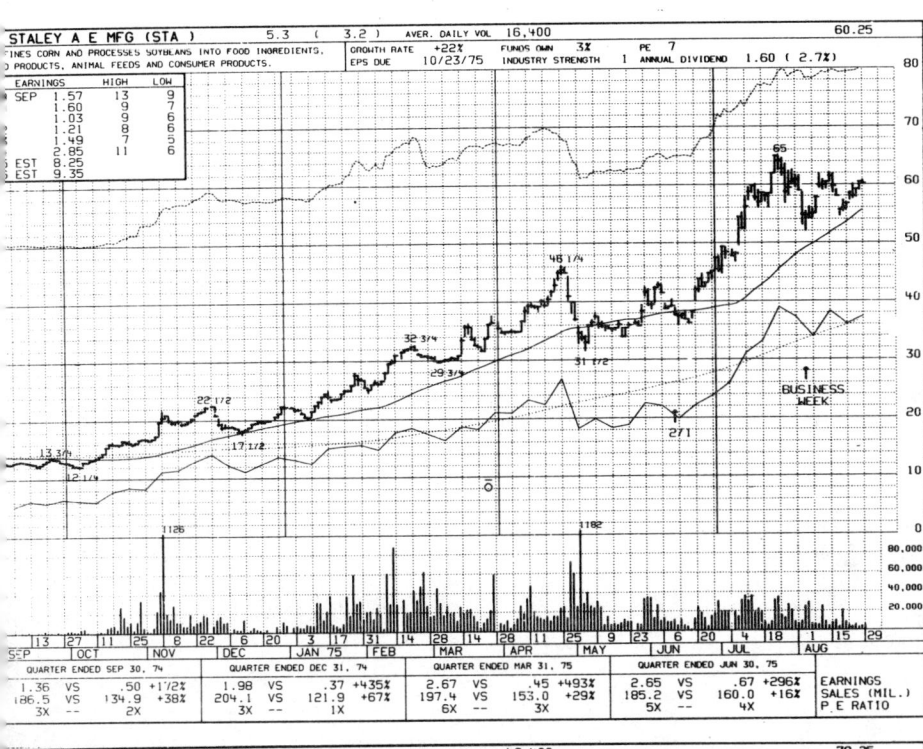
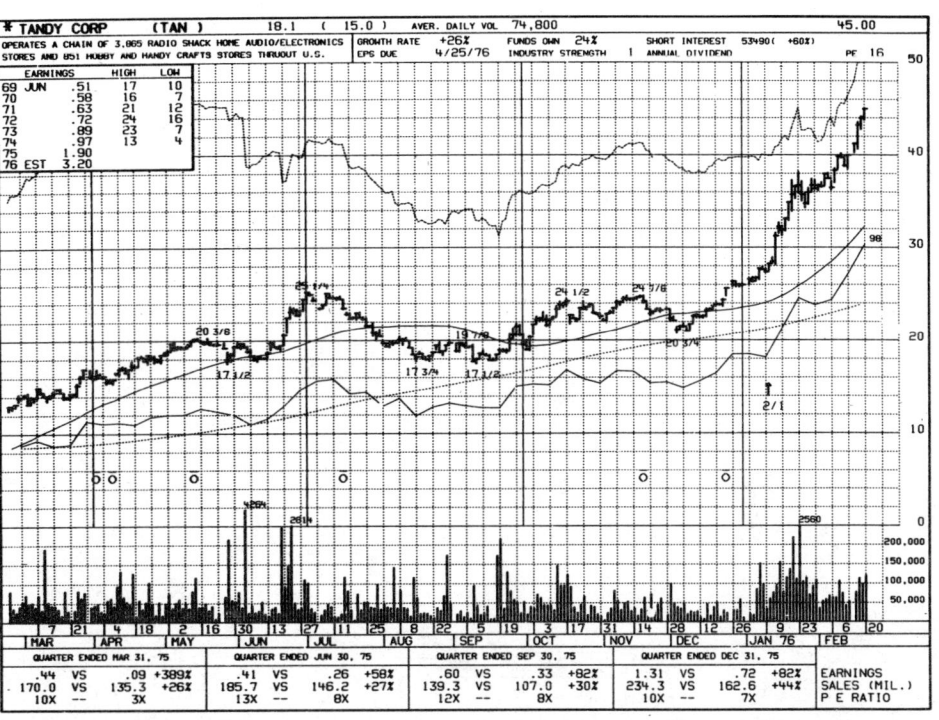
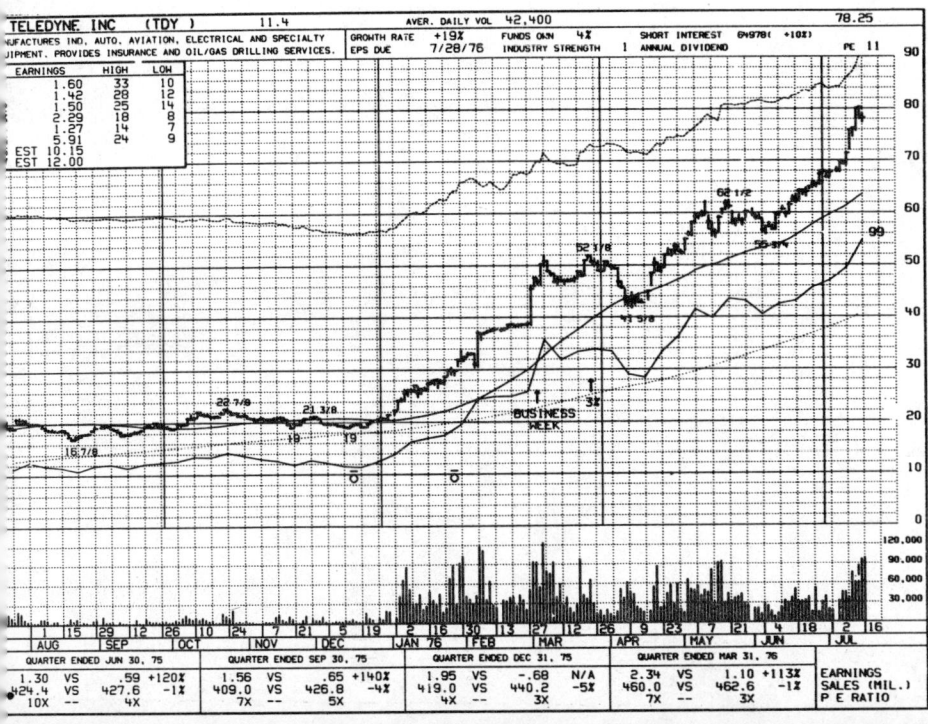
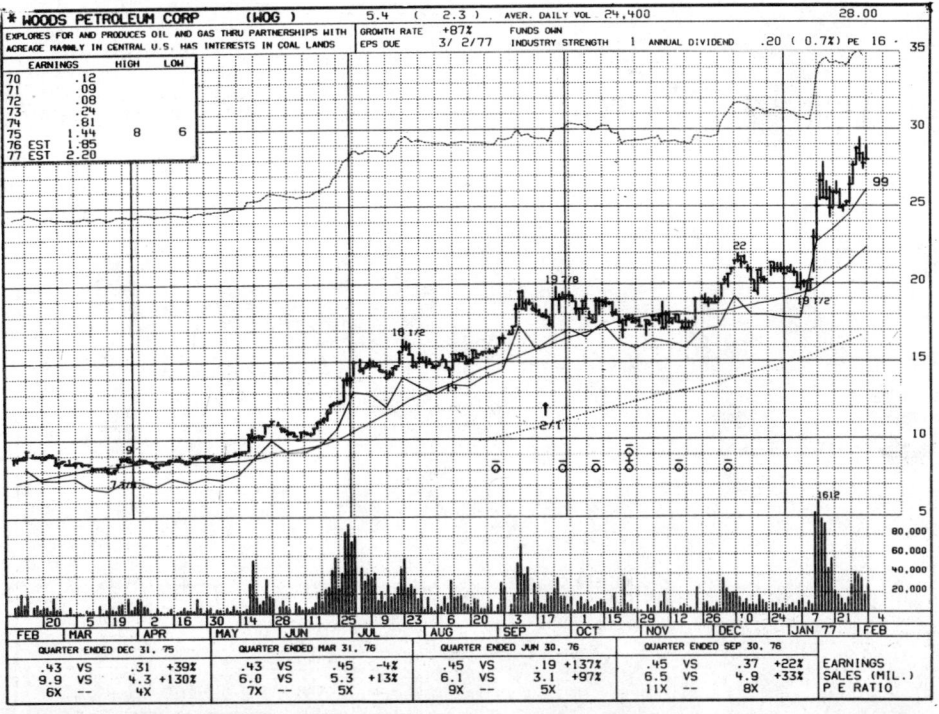